Jingo

also by Terry Pratchett, adapted by Stephen Briggs

THE FIFTH ELEPHANT
GOING POSTAL
INTERESTING TIMES
MONSTROUS REGIMENT
NIGHT WATCH
THE TRUTH

Terry Pratchett

Jingo

adapted by

Stephen Briggs

Methuen Drama

Published by Methuen 2005

1 3 5 7 9 10 8 6 4 2

First published in 2005 by
Methuen Publishing Limited
215 Vauxhall Bridge Road
London SW1V 1EJ

Methuen Publishing Limited Reg. No. 3543167

A CIP catalogue record for this book is available
from the British Library

ISBN 0 413 77446 5

Typeset by Country Setting, Kingsdown, Kent
Printed and bound in Great Britain by
Cox and Wyman Ltd, Reading, Berkshire

Introduction

All the Discworld's a Stage

The first people *ever* to dramatise the Discworld, in any form, were the Studio Theatre Club in Abingdon, Oxon. That was in 1991, with *Wyrd Sisters*.

We had already staged our own adaptations of other works: Monty Python's *Life of Brian* and *Holy Grail*, and Tom Sharpe's *Porterhouse Blue* and *Blott on the Landscape*. We were looking for something new when someone said 'Try Terry Pratchett – you'll like him'. So I ventured into the previously uncharted territory of the 'Fantasy' section of the local bookstore ('Here Be Dragons'). I read a Terry Pratchett book; I liked it. I read all of them. I wrote to Terry and asked if we could stage *Wyrd Sisters*. He said yes.

Wyrd Sisters sold out. So did *Mort* the year after.

So did *Guards! Guards!*, *Men at Arms*, and *Maskerade* in the years after that. In fact, 'sold out' is too modest a word. 'Oversold very quickly so that by the time the local newspaper mentioned it was on we'd had to close the booking office' is nearer the mark.

My casts were all happy enough to read whichever book we were staging, and to read others in the canon, too. The books stand on their own, but some knowledge of the wider Discworld ethos is essential when adapting the stories, and can also help directors to find out where it's all coming from, and the actors with their characterisations.

The Discworld novels have been getting longer (and darker) as the years pass and it is a problem to try to put over the plot while still meeting the overriding target for amdram – getting into the pub before closing. The important thing was to decide what was the basic plot: anything which didn't contribute to that was liable to be dropped in order to keep the play flowing. Favourite scenes, even favourite characters, have on occasions had to be dumped. These are hard decisions, but the book has to work as a *play*. You can't get four hundred pages of novel into two and a half hours on stage without sacrifices.

Each play also offers a challenge to directors in working out who can double for whom in order to stage them with a smaller cast. You'll see from the cast list which follows this introduction how *we* covered all the roles.

Although the majority of our audiences are 'fans', I've tried to remember when writing the plays that not *all* the audience will be steeped in Discworld lore. Some of them may just be normal theatregoers who've never read a fantasy novel in their whole lives – humorous fantasy may not be their 'thing', but I wouldn't want them to feel they were watching something which had been typed on an Enigma machine.

The books are episodic and have a sort of 'cinematic' construction; I have retained this format in *Jingo* and used different stage areas and levels with brisk lighting changes to keep the action flowing. Set changes slow down the action, even when they're really slick. A thirty-second blackout between each scene, accompanied by rustling, crashing and muffled swearing from your stage crew means you're in danger of losing the audience. Even *ten*-second changes, if repeated often enough, will lead to loss of interest. I've been to see many productions of the plays and the best have been those that have used bare stages or composite sets – leaving the majority of the 'scene-changing' to the lighting technician. The golden rule is: if you *can* do it without scene-shifting, *do* it without scene-shifting. It's a concept that has served radio drama very well (everyone *knows* that radio has the best scenery). And Shakespeare managed very well without it, too.

The plays do, however, call for some unusual props. Over the years, many of these have been made by my casts and crew: large hour-glasses for Death's house, shadow puppets, archaic rifles, dragon-scorched books, a church spire for *Jingo*. Other, more specialised props were put 'out to contract': Death's sword and scythe, an orang-utan, Detritus's head and hands, a Death of Rats, a Greebo, Scraps the dog and two swamp dragons (one an elaborate hand puppet and one with a fire-proof compartment in its bottom for a flight scene).

Since the Studio Theatre Club started the trend in 1991, Terry and I have had many enquiries about staging the plays – from as far afield as Finland, South Africa,

Indonesia, Australia, Bermuda and the Czech Republic (as well as Sheffield, Aberdeen, Exeter and the Isle of Man). One has even been staged in Antarctica! Royalties just from the five plays administered by me have raised over £50,000 so far for the Orangutan Foundation.

So how did our productions actually go? We enjoyed them. Our audiences seemed to enjoy them (after all, some of them were prepared, year after year, to travel down to Abingdon in Oxfordshire from Taunton, Newcastle-upon-Tyne, Ipswich, Basingstoke and . . . well, Oxford). Terry seems to enjoy them, too. He says that many of our members looked as though they had been recruited straight off the streets of Ankh-Morpork. He said that several of them were born to play the 'rude mechanicals' in Vitoller's troupe in *Wyrd Sisters*. He said that in his mind's eye the famous Ankh-Morpork City Watch *are* the players of the Studio Theatre Club.

I'm sure these were meant to be compliments.

Jingo

By the time we staged *Jingo* in 1997, we knew that the Discworld plays were a winner . . . though we'd learned that the flourishing trade in other groups staging the plays meant that we couldn't afford to take full houses for granted. They're still full, but we do have to work a bit now to achieve that.

As with all the adaptations, there were difficult choices about which scenes should be sacrificed to try and keep the play down to a reasonable running time. *Jingo* had a very complex plot and the version we staged in 1997 was quite lengthy. I have trimmed the script quite a bit, you will be pleased to hear, partly to simplify the plot slightly and partly to save a little time. Groups which are particularly keen to get to the pub earlier might also consider omitting Act One Scene Four. I like it because it introduces Nobby and Colon, but it does add nothing to the actual plot!

This dramatisation was written with Abingdon's medieval Unicorn Theatre's restrictions, and the number of players I expected to have available in mind. Really complicated

scenic effects were virtually impossible. Basically, we had a
bare stage with an onstage balcony at the back of the stage
and a small curtained area beneath it. Anyone thinking of
staging a Discworld play can be as imaginative as they like –
call upon the might of Industrial Light & Magic, if it's within
their budget. But *Jingo can* be staged with only a relatively
modest outlay on special effects. Bigger groups, with teams
of experts on hand, can let their imaginations run wild!

In short, though, our experience and that of other groups
is that it pays to work hard on getting the costumes and
lighting right, and to keep the scenery to little more than
perhaps a few changes of level enhanced by lighting effects
and carefully chosen background music. There's room for all
sorts of ideas here. The Discworld, as it says in the books, is
your mollusc.

Characterisation Within the constraints of what is known and
vital about each character, there is still room for flexibility
of interpretation. With the main roles, though, you have to
recognise that your audiences will expect them to look as
much like the book descriptions as possible. Most drama
clubs don't have a vast range from which to choose, though,
and it's the acting that's more important than the look of
the player when it comes down to it! There is some useful
character information about Vimes, Vetinari, Colon, Nobby,
Angua and some of the others in *The Discworld Companion*.

Costumes We played the 'present-day' scenes in a sort of
late-Victorian setting (though the City Watch retained their
English Civil War look throughout), with the Ankh-Morpork
soldiery having a red-coated Victorian look to them. The
Klatchians, of course, were a mix of *Arabian Nights* –
traditional Arab dress, 'belly dancers' and, of course, striped
shifts, sun glasses and fezzes for Colon and Vetinari.

Scenery Virtually none. Some bits of painted backing and
free-standing pedals for the submarine interior, cut-out boats
for the first scene . . . Apart from that, a virtually bare stage,
with occasional bits of furniture and hand-props.

Oh, and a word on pronunciation . . .   Having seen many of the plays staged, pronunciation of the names seems sometimes to be a stumbling block. Here are some pointers:

Ankh-Morpork   Ankh, as in 'bank', Morpork as in 'more pork', with the stress in the city's name on the second syllable – Ankh-*Mor*pork.

Vetinari   Long 'a' and stress the third syllable – Vetin*ah*-ri.

Angua   Hard 'g'. Either '*Ang*wa' or '*Ang*-you-ah' – stress on the first syllable for either.

Al Khali   Al *Kar*ley (yes, I do know it's a pun on 'alkali', but it doesn't work on stage).

Thinking of staging it?   Although Methuen control the amateur rights for *Jingo*, Terry and I are keen to know which of our plays are being staged where, so do feel free to write to me or email me with your production dates, just in case one of us can get to see your show. I also have some stocks of a snazzy City Watch badge. I have a website (www.StephenBriggs.com) or I can be contacted via Methuen, or direct by email (sbriggs@cix.co.uk).

Stephen Briggs
February 2005

Jingo

Characters

Lord Vetinari
Commander Vimes
Lady Sybil Ramkin
Captain Carrot
Sergeant Colon
Sergeant Detritus
General Ashal
Corporal Nobbs
Corporal Angua
Constable Shoe
Corporal Littlebottom
Lieutenant Hornett
Lord Rust
Les Jackson
Leonard of Quirm
Khufurah
Cadram
Mrs Spent
71-Hour Ahmed
Solid Jackson
The Dis-Organiser

Jabbar
Willikins
Greasy Arif
Footnote
Burleigh
The Librarian
Slant
Klatchian Ambassador
Akhan
Captain Jenkins
Downey
Mystic
Look-Out
Klatchian Captain
Traders
Al-Jibla
Bana
Netal
Mother-in-Law
Klatchian Man
Klatchian Guard

This dramatisation of *Jingo* was first presented by the Studio
Theatre Club at the Unicorn Theatre, Abingdon, on
2 December 1997, with the following cast:

Lord Vetinari	Stephen Briggs
Commander Vimes	Trevor Collins
Lady Sybil Ramkin	Sharon Stone
Captain Carrot	Mark Cowper
Sergeant Colon	Keith Franklin
Sergeant Detritus/	
General Ashal	Mike Allum
Corporal Nobbs	Graham Cook
Corporal Angua	Kath Leighton
Constable Shoe/	
Lieutenant Hornett	Robin Allen
Lord Rust/Les Jackson	Tim Arnot
Leonard of Quirm	John Kirchhoff
Khufurah	Annie Davis
Cadram/Mrs Spent	Claire Spittlehouse
71-Hour Ahmed/	
Solid Jackson	Colin Macnee
The Disorganiser	Jacqui Hill
Jabbar	Mike Davey
Willikins/Greasy Arif	Andrew Bailey
Footnote/Burleigh	Antonia Bremble
The Librarian/Slant	Claire Aston
Klatchian Ambassador/	
Akhan	Dominic Plunkett
Captain Jenkins	Phil Evans

Other roles played by memebers of the cast.

Directed by	Stephen Briggs
Lighting by	Colin James
Stage Management	Phil Evans
	and Dominic Plunkett
Sound by	Catherine Long

Act One

Scene One

The Circle Sea.

Midway between Ankh-Morpork and Klatch. The lights come up and we see a small fishing boat with its crew of **Solid** *and* **Les Jackson**.

Solid Jackson   Not a thing in half an hour.

Les Jackson   You sure we're in the right spot, Dad?

Solid Jackson   Course. You can see the lights of Al-Khali over there, and of Ankh-Morpork over there. Halfway between. Can't work out why we haven't caught anything yet.

Pause. Water lapping. Thunder.

Mind you . . . I reckon we ought to be getting out of here. Got a bit of a funny feeling.

Les Jackson   What're we going to use for wind, Dad?

Splash of oars.

Solid Jackson (*standing in the boat and looking, off*)   I knows that's you, you thieving bastard!

Greasy Arif (*off*)   May you be consumed by a thousand devils, you damned person!

Solid Jackson   Fished 'em all out, have you? You thieving foreign bastard!

Greasy Arif (*off*)   My curvy sword at your neck, you unclean son of a dog of the female persuasion!

Les Jackson (*who has been looking over the side of the boat*)   Dad?

Solid Jackson   That's Greasy Arif out there! You take a good look at him! He's been coming out here for years, stealing our catch.

Les Jackson   Dad, there's . . .

Solid Jackson   You get on them oars and I'll knock his black teeth out! Come on, row!

Les Jackson   I can't, Dad! We're stuck on something!

Solid Jackson   It's a hundred fathoms deep, here. What's there to stick on?

Les Jackson   It looks like . . . a chicken, Dad.

Muffled sound of church bell ringing.

Solid Jackson   Chickens can't swim!

Les Jackson (*reaching into the water*)   It's made of iron, Dad!

A weathercock rises out of the water upstage of the boat.

Solid Jackson (*holding up a lantern to it*)   What the . . . ? Quick! Quick! Row like hell, boy! Come on!

Les Jackson   But why? What is it?

Solid Jackson   It's a bloody weathercock, isn't it? It's the lost kingdom of Leshp! I think it's found it's way back!

Klaxon. **Footnote** *enters to spot. Also, in the dark, the following characters enter –* **Lord Vetinari**, **Commander Vimes**, **Captain Carrot**, **Corporal Angua**, **Leonard of Quirm** *and the* **Librarian**.

Footnote   Good evening. I'm sorry to pause the show at this exciting juncture, but I think perhaps I should introduce you to the world on which our play is set and to some of the principal characters in our tale. This is Discworld. Circular and flat. Like a geological pizza, but without the anchovies. It is carried through space on the backs of four huge elephants, who themselves stand on the back of a cosmically large turtle, the Great A'Tuin. On a world such as this, which exists because the gods enjoy a joke as much as the next super-entity, anything can happen. Most of our story takes place in the principal city of Discworld, Ankh-Morpork. Ankh-Morpork is run by the Patrician, Lord Vetinari.

Pin spot on **Vetinari**.

Lord Vetinari is a true democrat. He believes in the principle of one man, one vote. He's the man. He's got the vote. He rules the city with an iron hand in a velvet glove. He is assisted in this by Commander Sir Samuel Vimes of the City Watch.

Pin spot on **Vimes**.

Commander Vimes hates authority in any form. One of his ancestors beheaded the last King of Ankh-Morpork and Commander Vimes thinks that was a damn good job, too. Commander Vimes cares for the city as much as Lord Vetinari, but in a different way. Lord Vetinari cares for it as if it were a piece of delicate machinery; Vimes cares about the people. Vimes's first officer in the Watch is Captain Carrot.

Pin spot up on **Carrot**.

Carrot is the rightful heir to the throne of Ankh-Morpork. But he doesn't want the job. He likes being a Watchman and he's taken great pains to hide all evidence of his royal lineage. He is honest, straightforward and scrupulously fair. Oh, and perhaps four other characters need a little bit of introduction.

Pin spots up on **Angua**.

Corporal Angua and Captain Carrot are, erm, an *item*. She was not only the first woman to be appointed to the City Watch, but she is also the Watch's first *werewolf*. A nice girl, but best not to irritate during full moon. Since gaining a werewolf, the Watch has gone on to recruit dwarfs, trolls, vampires and even a zombie.

Pin spot up on **Leonard**.

Leonard of Quirm here is a genius. He is one of the Disc's great thinkers and inventors. He invents everything and anything. Though he wouldn't harm a soul, some of his inventions could be used for harm. So Lord Vetinari keeps him well out of harm's way. Oh, and this is the Librarian of Unseen University –

Pin spot up on the **Librarian**.

– the Discworld's premier college of wizardry. He was transformed into an orangutan during a magical explosion and resists all efforts to turn him back. Basically, his current form is easier for reaching the high shelves, and his problems are limited to 'Where's the next banana coming from?'

She hands him a banana. All pin spots off.

Now then, back to the plot.

Behind her, buildings rise out of the water, slowly. On the screen, a civic skyline rises and swamps the two boats.

You might expect that the sudden appearance of a city that disappeared into the sea hundreds of years ago would be accompanied by tidal waves, expensive special effects and so on. There was not, on the whole, a lot of geological excitement. No volcanoes, hurricanes, earthquakes. No. The miraculous reappearance of the Lost Kingdom of Leshp, which sank thousands of years ago, caused only a five foot wave to reach the circular shores of the Circle Sea.

Klaxon. She exits. Sound of rushing water, followed by dripping sounds.

Les Jackson (*looking around*)   It's a city, Dad!

Greasy Arif (*entering, on foot*)   You foolish man!

Solid Jackson (*getting out of the boat, waving an oar*)   Don't you touch anything! This land belongs to Ankh-Morpork!

Greasy Arif   I claim this land for the Serif of Al-Khali!

Solid Jackson   We saw it first. Les, you tell him we saw it first!

Greasy Arif   We saw it first before you saw it first! See the untrustworthy way he attacks us, Akhan!

Solid Jackson   Get those filthy sandals off Ankh-Morporkian territory!

Greasy Arif   He has set foot on Klatchian soil! The fish thief!

Les Jackson   Dad, come on! It's not that important. I mean, who cares who saw it first, eh? We're both hundreds of miles from home. I mean, who's going to *know*, Dad?

Solid Jackson (*aside to* **Les**)   Who's going to know? The people who greet the first boat back with the news, that's who! (*Loudly, for* **Arif***'s benefit.*) The lad's right. Daft to argue.

He starts to push his boat offstage. **Les** *and* **Akhan** *examine the buildings and so on.*

Greasy Arif   Indeed.

He has clearly come to the same conclusion. Keeping his eyes on **Solid***, he reaches for* **Akhan***'s arm, but grabs* **Les***'s. At the same time,* **Solid** *reaches for* **Les***'s arm but grabs* **Akhan***'s.* **Arif** *and* **Solid** *start to exit, both realise their error and swap sons.*

Arif *and* **Solid**   So – trying to take my son! A kidnapper as well, eh?

They grab their own sons and start to exit as the lights black out.

Scene Two

Sator Square, Ankh-Morpork.

On stage is a small crowd watching a speaker on a soap box – **Captain Jenkins**. **Commander Vimes** *and* **Sergeant Detritus** *enter to the back of the crowd.*

Captain Jenkins   . . . It's time they were taught a lesson! Why don't our so-called masters listen to the voice of the people? Ankh-Morpork has had enough of these swaggering brigands from Klatch! They steal our fish, they steal our trade and now they're stealing our lands!

Murmurs of approval from the crowd.

They stole my merchandise! It's a bloody pirate empire! I was boarded! In Ankh-Morpork waters! They stole a cargo of fine silks!

Vimes   Ah. Not dried fish offal and condemned meat, then? That's your normal cargo, I believe, Captain Jenkins.

Captain Jenkins *(not quite sure who spoke)*   Fine silks! And what does the city care about that? Nothing!

Cries of 'Shame!' from the crowd.

Vimes   Has the city been *told*?

Captain Jenkins   Er . . . well, it's. Um. Er . . . I –

Vimes   *I* care. Shouldn't be too hard to track down a cargo of fine silks that stinks of fish-guts.

Laughter from the crowd.

Detritus, just go along with Captain Jenkins here, will you? His ship is the *Milka*, I believe. He'll show you all the lading bills and manifests and receipts and things.

Detritus   Yessir!

Captain Jenkins   Er . . . you can't. They, er, they stole the paperwork as well.

Vimes   Really? So they can take it back to the shop if it doesn't fit?

Laughter from crowd.

Captain Jenkins   Er . . . anyway, the ship's sailed. Yes, sailed! Got to try and recoup my losses, you know!

Vimes   Sailed? Without its Captain? So Mr Scoplett is in charge? Your first officer?

Captain Jenkins   Yes, yes.

Vimes *(snapping his fingers theatrically)*   Damn! Then that man we've got in the cells on a charge of being Naughtily Drunk last night . . . we're going to have to charge him with impersonation as well, then? I don't know . . . more blasted paperwork.

Captain Jenkins   I'll, er . . . I'll go and sort . . . I'd better go and . . . er . . .

He exits, hurriedly.

Detritus   You want I should go and 'ave a look at 'is boat?

Vimes   No. That won't be necessary. There won't be any silk and there won't be any paperwork. There won't be anything except a lingering aroma of fish-guts.

Detritus   Wow, dem damn Klatchians steals everything that ain't nailed down, right?

Vimes   They don't have trolls in Klatch, do they?

Detritus   Nossir. It's der heat. Troll brains don't work well in der heat. If I was to go to Klatch . . . I'd be really *stoopid*.

Vimes   Detritus?

Detritus   Yessir?

Vimes   Never go to Klatch.

Detritus   Nossir.

One of the departing crowd has left a banner with the legend GREASY FORANE HANDS OFF LESHP.

Leshp. Now dere's a name that ain't got its teeth in.

Vimes   It's the land that came back up from the sea last week. There's speakers all over the city insisting that we have a duty to protect our countrymen on this refound land.

Detritus   'Ere, 'ow come there's 'countrymen' on this newfoundland if it only come out of der sea last week? They bin 'olding their breff?

Vimes   A good question. There's a nasty mood in the air. We've been at peace with Klatch for nearly a century. We're neighbours, for gods' sakes. But now, some damn rock has risen out of the sea and everyone's acting like Klatch hasn't returned our lawnmower.

Corporal Nobbs *runs on.*

Vimes   Yes, Nobby, what is it?

Nobby   Glad I found you, sir. The Patrician wants to see you. He said he 'requires your attendance'.

Vimes   Oh does he? Good.

Blackout.

Scene Three

The Patrician's Palace.

On stage are **Vetinari**, **Downey** *of the Assassins' Guild, Mr* **Burleigh** *of the Armourers' Guild,* **Slant** *of the Lawyers' Guild,* **Lord Rust** *and whatever other civic dignitaries you can muster.* **Downey** *is just concluding a long exposition of the value of the Assassins' Guild.*

Downey   . . . and in conclusion, and to keep my promise to be brief . . .

Rust   Too late.

Downey   . . . I would stress that we in the Guild of Assassins offer a very high level of training to our student assassins and we are of high value to the City.

Lord Vetinari   Well, thank you, Downey. I am sure we will all sleep easier in our beds for knowing all that. Just one minor point . . . I believe the word 'assassin' actually comes from Klatch?

Downey   Well . . . indeed . . . um?

Lord Vetinari   And I believe also that many of your students are from Klatch and its neighbouring countries . . . ?

Downey   The unrivalled quality of our education . . .

Lord Vetinari   Quite so. So you have said. Extensively. What you are telling me, in point of fact, is that their assassins have been doing it longer, know their way around our city and have had their skills honed by you?

Downey   Er . . .

Lord Vetinari   We surely have superiority in weapons, Burleigh? Do give me your reassurance, as the Head of the Armourers' Guild.

Burleigh   Oh yes. We've been turning out some superb stuff recently. (*He clears his throat, awkwardly.*) But the thing is . . .

Lord Vetinari   Yes. The thing is, as I imagine you were about to tell me, is that the important thing about the weapons business is that it is a business. Mm?

Burleigh   Er . . . yes.

Lord Vetinari   That, in fact, weapons are for selling?

Burleigh   Er . . . exactly.

Lord Vetinari   To anyone who wishes to buy them?

Burleigh   Er . . . yes.

Lord Vetinari   And I expect that in recent years a very lucrative market has been Klatch?

Burleigh   Well, yes . . . the Serif needed to pacify the outlying regions . . .

But **Vetinari** *has held up his hand.* **Burleigh** *stops speaking.* **Vetinari** *refers to a piece of paper in his hand.*

Lord Vetinari   The 'Great Leveller Cart-Mounted Ten-Bank 500-Pound Crossbow'? And, let me see . . . the 'Meteor Automated Throwing Star Hurler − Decapitates at Twenty Paces, Money Back If Not Completely Decapitated'?

Burleigh   Have you ever heard of the D'regs, my Lord? Fierce desert tribesmen. They say the only way to pacify one of *them* is to hit them repeatedly with an axe and bury what's left under a rock. And even then, choose a heavy rock.

Vetinari *seems to be studying the weapons list.*

Erm . . . besides, we provide much-needed jobs in Ankh-Morpork.

Lord Vetinari   Exporting these weapons to other countries.

He smiles and hands the paper to **Burleigh**.

I'm very pleased to see that the industry has done so well. I will bear this particularly in mind. The situation is grave, ladies and gentlemen. A number of our citizens have gone out to this wretched island of Leshp. As have, I understand, a number of Klatchians.

Rust   But why are our people going out there?

Lord Vetinari *(taking a note from* **Drumknott** *and reading from it)*   Because they are showing a brisk pioneering spirit and seeking additional wealth in a new land.

Downey   What's in it for the Klatchians?

Lord Vetinari *(again, referring to his notes)*   Oh, they've gone out there because they are a bunch of unprincipled opportunists always ready to grab something for nothing.

Burleigh   A masterly summing up, if I may say so, my Lord.

Lord Vetinari   Oh, I do beg your pardon. I seem to have read those two sentences in the wrong order.

Mr Slant, I believe you have something to say here?

Slant *(referring to a heavy, leather-bound book)*   Yes indeed. The history of the Kingdom of Leshp is a little obscure. It is known to have been above the sea almost a thousand years ago, when legal records suggest that it was considered a part of the Ankh-Morpork Empire.

Vimes *enters.*

Lord Vetinari   What is the nature of these records and do they say *who* considered Leshp to be a part of our Empire?

Ah, Vimes. Glad you could make it.

Slant   The records date back several hundred years, my Lord. But of course, they are *our* legal records.

Lord Vetinari   Only ours?

Slant   I hardly think that others could apply.

Vimes   Klatchian ones, for example?

Slant   The Klatchians, Sir Samuel? The Klatchian language does not even have a word for lawyer.

Vimes   Good for them.

Slant   It is our view that the new land is ours by Eminent Domain, under the ancient law of Acquiris Quodcumque Rapis.

Vimes   Hold on. 'Acquiris' . . . ? 'You Get What You Grab'? That's it?

Slant   I am given to understand that it was one of our fishermen who first set foot on the new land.

Lord Vetinari   I believe the Klatchians make a similar claim.

Slant   Surely, my lord, you wouldn't just take their word for it? I can't believe that proud Ankh-Morpork is going to be told what to do by a bunch of thieves with towels on their heads.

Rust   No, indeed. It's time Johnny Klatchian was taught a lesson. Look at that business last year with the cabbages. Ten damn boat-loads they wouldn't accept!

Vimes   And everyone knows that caterpillars add to the flavour.

Rust That's right! Good honest protein! And you remember all that trouble Captain Jenkins had with that cargo of mutton? They were going to *imprison* him! In a *Klatchian* jail!

Vimes Surely not? Meat is at its best when it's turning green.

Burleigh It's not as though they could taste the difference under all that curry. I was at a dinner at their embassy once. You know what they tried to make me eat? It was a sheep's . . . well, it was a sheep's, erm . . .

Lord Vetinari Yes, thank you, Burleigh. I think we are straying from the point.

Rust Send in a damn warship. Like in the old days. Put a few shots over their bows.

Lord Vetinari Rust, these are *not* the old days. In any case, we do not have an army. I am not a great military man, but I believe one of those is generally considered vital to the prosecution of a successful war. The city historically has been violently opposed to a standing army.

Downey And we all know why the city doesn't trust an army. A lot of armed men, standing around with nothing to do . . . they start to get ideas . . .

Downey, **Rust**, **Burleigh** *and* **Slant** *all turn to look at* **Vimes**.

Vimes (*with heavy irony*) My word. Can this be a reference to 'Old Stoneface' Vimes, who led the city's militia in a revolt against the rule of a tyrannical monarch in order to bring some sort of freedom and justice to the place? I do believe it is. And wasn't he the Commander of the Watch at the time? Good Heavens, I believe he was! And isn't he an ancestor of the current Commander? Well, blow me down, coincidence piles on coincidence, doesn't it? Right. So that's out of the way. Now, does anyone actually have a *point* they want to make?

A general embarrassed clearing of throats.

Slant   What about mercenaries?

Lord Vetinari   We cannot afford mercenaries.

Downey   How can this be? Don't we pay our taxes?

Lord Vetinari   Ah. I thought we might come to that.

He takes a list from **Drumknott**.

Let me see now . . . ah yes. Guild of Assassins. Gross
earnings in the last year AM$13,207,048. Taxes paid in the
last year – forty seven dollars and twenty-two pence.

Downey   That's all perfectly legal. The Guild of
Accountants said . . .

Lord Vetinari   Ah yes. Guild of Accountants. Gross
earnings AM$7,999,011. Taxes paid: nil. But I see they
applied for a rebate of AM$200,000.

Taxation, gentlemen, is very much like dairy farming. The
task is to extract the maximum amount of milk with the
minimum amount of moo. I fear all I get these days is the
moo.

Downey   Are you telling us that Ankh-Morpork is
bankrupt?

Lord Vetinari   Of course. Whilst at the same time, full of
rich people.

Rust   Wholesale tax avoidance? That is a disgusting state
of affairs!

Lord Vetinari   Commander Vimes?

Vimes   Sir?

Lord Vetinari   Would you be so good as to assemble a
squad of your most experienced men, liaise with the tax
gatherers and obtain the accumulated back taxes, please. My
clerk, Drumknott, can give you a list of the defaulters.

Vimes   Right, sir. And if they resist . . . ?

Lord Vetinari But how can they? This is the will of our civic leaders.

He takes a list from **Drumknott**.

Let me see, now. Top of the list . . .

Rust *(hurriedly)* Er . . . far too late for that sort of thing now.

Downey Water under the bridge.

Slant Dead and buried. So to speak.

Vimes *(virtuously)* I paid mine.

Lord Vetinari So let me recap, then. I don't think anyone wants to see two grown nations scrapping over a piece of rock. We don't want to fight, but . . .

Rust . . . by jingo, if we do, we'll show those . . .

Lord Vetinari We have no ships. We have no men. We have no money, too. Of course we *do* have the art of diplomacy. You'd be amazed what can be achieved with just a few words.

Rust We don't have to talk to these people! It's up to us to show them that we won't be pushed around! We must re-form the regiments!

Vimes Oh, *private* armies? Under the command of someone whose fitness for it lies in the fact that he can afford a thousand funny hats?

Rust Whose fitness, *Mister* Vimes, lies in a thousand years of breeding for leadership.

Vimes Ah, good breeding. No, sorry, don't have any of that, if that's what you need to get a lot of men killed . . .

Lord Vetinari Gentlemen, please. Let's have no fighting please. This is, after all, a council of war. As for re-forming the regiments. Well, this is your ancient right . . .

Vimes You're going to *let* them play soldiers?

Burleigh   Oh, Commander Vimes, as a military man yourself . . .

Vimes (*dangerously calm*)   I am not a military man.

Burleigh   Surely . . . armour? Sword? Helmet? It's all the same, isn't it?

Vimes   No. It's not.

Lord Vetinari   I can only repeat that tomorrow I shall be talking with Prince Khufurah . . .

Rust   I've heard good reports of him. Strict but fair. One can only admire what he's achieved in some of the backward regions . . .

Lord Vetinari   No, you are thinking of Prince Cadram. Khufurah is the younger brother. He is arriving as his brother's special envoy.

Rust   Him? He's a wastrel, a cheat. It's said he takes bri . . .

Lord Vetinari   Thank you for your diplomatic input, Rust. There is always a way. Our nations have many interests in common. Prince Cadram is clearly taking this very seriously if he is sending his own brother to deal with it.

Vimes   A Klatchian bigwig is coming here? No one told me!

Lord Vetinari   Strange as it may seem, Sir Samuel, I am occasionally capable of governing this city for minutes at a time without seeking your advice and guidance.

Vimes   I meant, there's a lot of anti-Klatchian feeling around . . .

Lord Vetinari   I am sure you will see to it that the streets are safe to walk, Vimes. I know you take a pride in that. Officially, he is here at the wizards' invitation. To receive an honorary doctorate. I believe we have finished, ladies and gentlemen. Don't let me take any more of your valuable time.

They all leave, except **Vimes**, *who lurks.*

You appear to be casting a shadow, Vimes.

Vimes You're not really going to allow them to re-form the regiments are you, my lord?

Lord Vetinari There is absolutely no law against it, Vimes. And it will keep them occupied. Every official gentleman is required to raise an army if the city requires it.

Vimes Yes, but you see, sir, I can't help thinking that over there in Klatch there's another bunch of idiots doing the same thing.

Lord Vetinari Thank you, Commander. Well, I mustn't keep you from that massive pile of paperwork on your desk. I imagine I will see you tomorrow at the Convivium.

Vimes Sir?

Lord Vetinari The Unseen University degree ceremony. As you know, the Commander of the City Watch leads the procession in full dress uniform.

Vimes Wha . . . ?

Lord Vetinari Lady Sybil assured me that you would be there with a crisp bright shiny morning face.

Vimes You asked my wife?

Lord Vetinari Certainly. She is very proud of you. She believes you are capable of great things. She must be a great comfort to you.

Vimes Well, I . . . er, that is . . . um . . . yes, sir.

Lord Vetinari Splendid.

Blackout.

Scene Four

The Dockside, Ankh-Morpork.

Corporal Nobbs *and* **Sergeant Colon** *stand, idly watching dockside workers (off). Lapping water effects.*

Nobby You ever been to sea, Sarge?

Colon Hah, not me. You can't bloody trust the sea. Treacherous.

Nobby My mum's uncle was a sailor. But after the big plague he got press-ganged. Bunch of farmers got him drunk. He woke up next morning tied to a plough.

Pause.

What d'you reckon to this trouble with Klatch then, eh, Sarge?

Colon Won't last long. Lot of cowards, the Klatchians. The moment they taste a bit of cold steel they're legging it over the sand.

Nobby Shouldn't be any trouble to sort out, then?

Colon And o' course, they're not the same colour as what we are. Well . . . as me, anyway. Know how you can tell a Klatchian? You look and see if he used a lot of words starting with 'al', right? Cos that's a dead giveaway. They invented all the words beginning with 'al'. That's how you can tell they're Klatchian. Like al-cohol, see?

Nobby They invented beer?

Colon Yeah.

Nobby That's clever.

Colon More luck, I'd say.

Nobby What else did they do?

Colon Well . . . there's . . . there's al-gebra. That's like sums with letters, for . . . for people whose brains aren't clever enough for numbers, see?

Nobby I heard they've got a lot of odd gods.

Colon Yeah, and mad priests . . .

Nobby So how's that different? I mean, some of *our* priests are a bit on the batty side.

Colon I hope you're not being *unpatriotic*, Nobby.

Nobby No, of course not. No, I can see theirs'd be a lot worse, what with being foreign and so on.

Colon And, of course, they're all mad for fighting.

Nobby You mean, like they viciously attack you while cowardly running away after tasting cold steel?

Colon Hmph. You can't trust 'em, like I said. And they burp hugely after meals.

Nobby Well, so do you, Sarge.

Colon Yes, but I don't pretend it's *polite*, Nobby.

Nobby It's certainly a good job there's you around to explain things, Sarge. It's amazing the stuff you know.

Colon I surprise myself sometimes.

Scene Five

A room in Unseen University.

Vimes *is on stage, in most of his dress uniform. He is shaving. He already has a couple of bits of tissue stuck on his face.* **Willikins**, *the butler, enters.*

Willikins (*clears throat discreetly*) I think we had better proceed with alacrity, Sir Samuel. I have brought the rest of your dress uniform. You left it at the house, sir. I am sure it was an error.

Vimes Oh. Er. Thank you, Willikins.

Willikins You are due downstairs at the sherry party in fifteen minutes, sir. Lady Sybil has vouchsafed to me that if you are not there she will utilise your intestines for hosiery accessories, sir.

Vimes   Was she smiling?

Willikins   Only slightly, sir.

Vimes   Oh gods . . .

Willikins   *Yes*, sir.

Vimes *nicks himself with the razor.*

Vimes   Damn!

Willikins   I shall fetch some more tissue paper directly, sir.

Vimes   Did you pass on my message to Sergeant Colon?

Willikins   About getting Corporal Nobbs to rescue you from the sherry party? Yes, sir. (*He clears his throat discreetly.*) I should like to take this opportunity to raise a matter of some import, sir.

Vimes   Yes?

Willikins   Regretfully, I am afraid I must ask leave to give in my notice, sir. I wish to join the colours.

Vimes   Which colours are those, Willikins? Oh, you mean you want to join the army?

Willikins   They say Klatch needs to be taught a sharp lesson, sir. A Willikins has never been found wanting when his country calls. I thought that Lord Venturi's Heavy Infantry would do for me. They have a particularly attractive scarlet uniform, sir.

Vimes   You've had military experience, have you?

Willikins   Oh, no, sir. But I am a quick learner, sir, and I believe I have some prowess with a carving knife.

Vimes   On turkeys . . .

Willikins   Yes, sir.

Vimes   And you're off to fight the screaming hordes in Klatch, are you?

Willikins If it should come to that, sir.

Vimes Very sandy. So they say.

Willikins So I am led to believe, sir.

Vimes And rocky. Very rocky. Lots of rocks. Dusty too.

Willikins Very parched in parts, sir.

Vimes And so in this land of sand, sand-coloured dust
and sand-coloured rocks, you, Willikins, will march in with
your carving knife and your bright red uniform?

Willikins Yes, sir. If the need arises.

Vimes You don't see anything wrong with this picture?

Willikins Sir?

Vimes Oh, never mind. We shall miss you, Willikins.

Willikins Oh, Lord Venturi says it will be over by
Hogswatch.

Vimes Really? I didn't know it had even started.

Willikins What, sir?

Vimes Oh nothing. Thank you, Willikins, you can go.

Willikins Thank you, sir.

As **Willikins** *leaves,* **Lady Ramkin** *breezes in.*

Willikins My lady.

Lady Ramkin Ah, Willikins. Still in mufti?

Willikins Er, yes, my lady.

And he leaves.

Lady Ramkin Sam. Good, you're up and about.
Thought you might be dozin' in some side room.

Vimes No, no, my dear. As you see, I'm ready for the off.

Lady Ramkin And you *will* try to look dignified, won't
you?

Vimes   Yes, dear.

Lady Ramkin   What will you try to look?

Vimes   Dignified, dear.

Lady Ramkin   And *please* try to be diplomatic.

Vimes   Yes, dear.

Lady Ramkin   What will you try to be?

Vimes   Diplomatic, dear.

Lady Ramkin   You're using your 'henpecked' voice, Sam.

Vimes   Yes, dear.

Lady Ramkin   You know that's not fair.

Vimes   No, dear. All right, all *right*. It's just all this . . .
finery. I mean, supposing someone sees me?

Lady Ramkin   Of course they'll see you. You're leading
the procession. And I will be very proud of you. Here – (*She
produces a small package.*) A present for you, Sam. To help you
be more organised.

Vimes *opens it. It is a small box. He opens it and a demon pops
up. (We had our demon in a pin spot above and to one side of the
stage.)*

Disorganiser   Bingly, Bingly, Beep! Good day to you,
insert name here!

Vimes *slams it shut.*

Vimes   What on earth is it?

Lady Ramkin   It's a Disorganiser. It helps you organise
your appointments. That's why it's called an Organiser.

Vimes   It says *Dis*-organiser.

Lady Ramkin   Ah yes, well, the Dis bit means it's
operated by a small demon. A Dis. Have fun with it. The
man in the shop programmed some of it. Here's the
operating manual for it.

She hands over two large books.

Right, now come on, the sherry party's already in full swing.

Vimes   Oh good.

The lights change to the full stage, where various dignitaries are standing around, sipping sherry and chatting. By one doorway is **Corporal Nobbs**. **Vimes** *and* **Lady Ramkin** *enter. She mingles immediately.* **Vimes** *sidles over to* **Corporal Nobbs**.

Vimes   All quiet, Nobby?

Nobby   Yessir.

Vimes   Nothing going on at *all*?

Nobby   Nossir.

Vimes   What, nowhere? Nothing? There was trouble all over yesterday!

Nobby   Yessir.

Vimes   Fred Colon does know he can summon me if anything important happens, doesn't he?

Nobby   Oh, yessir.

Vimes   The Shades? There's always something . . .

Nobby   Dead quiet, sir.

Vimes   Damn. I suppose you couldn't take a brick and . . .

Nobby   Lady Sybil was very spiffic about how you was to stay here, sir.

Vimes   Spiffic?

Nobby   Yessir. She had a *word* with me. She give me a dollar.

Lady Ramkin *crosses the room to them. She is followed by the* **Prince Khufurah** *and* **71-Hour Ahmed**.

Lady Ramkin   Ah, Samuel, there you are. I don't think you've met the Prince Khufurah, have you? Highness, this is

Sir Samuel Vimes, Commander of the Ankh-Morpork City Watch.

Prince Khufurah   Sir Samuel. My carpet only got in two hours ago.

Vimes   Carpet? Oh, yes, of course. You flew.

Prince Khufurah   Yes. Very chilly, and of course you can't get a good meal. And did you get your man, Sir Samuel?

Vimes   What? Pardon?

Prince Khufurah   I believe our ambassador told me that you had to leave the reception last week quite suddenly . . . ?

Vimes   What? Oh. Yes. Yes, we got 'em all right.

Prince Khufurah   Well done. He put up a fight, I see.

Vimes *looks vague.* **Prince Khufurah** *taps his own jaw to indicate* **Vimes**' *shaving tissue.*

Vimes   Ah . . . er, yes.

Prince Khufurah   Commander Vimes always gets his man.

Vimes   Well, I wouldn't say I . . .

Prince Khufurah   Vetinari's terrier, I've heard them call you. Always hot on the chase, they say, and won't let go. In fact, it is fortuitous that I have met you, Commander.

Vimes   It is?

Prince Khufurah   I was just wondering at the meaning of the word shouted at my bodyguard as we were on our way down here. Would you be so kind?

Vimes   Erm . . . well . . .

Prince Khufurah   I believe it was . . . let me see now . . . oh, yes . . . 'towelhead'.

Vimes   It, er, refers to your national headdress.

Prince Khufurah   Oh. Is it some kind of obscure joke?

Vimes *(with a slight, resigned sigh)*   No. It's an insult.

Prince Khufurah   Ah? Well, we cannot be responsible for the ramblings of idiots, can we? I must commend you, Commander, on the breadth of your knowledge.

Vimes   I'm sorry?

Prince Khufurah   Yes. I must have asked a dozen people that question this morning and, do you know? Not *one* of them knew what it meant. And they *all* seemed to have caught a cough.

71-Hour Ahmed *laughs, very close to* **Vimes**. **Vimes** *reels at the smell of cloves on his breath. Embarrassed pause.*

Vimes   So. Are we going to have a scrap over this Leshp business or what?

Prince Khufurah   Pah. A few square miles of uninhabited fertile ground with superb anchorage in an unsurpassed strategic position? What sort of inconsequence is that for civilised people to war over?

Vimes   Sorry. I'm not good at this diplomacy business. Did you *mean* what you said just then?

Prince Khufurah   I don't believe you've met 71-Hour Ahmed, have you?

71-Hour Ahmed   Offendi.

Vimes   That's . . . er . . . an unusual name.

Prince Khufurah   Not at all. In my country Ahmed is a very common name.

Vimes   Do you have toothache, Mr, er . . . Ahmed?

71-Hour Ahmed   No, offendi. It is a clove. We chew them. Another of our strange foreign traditions.

He laughs. **Vimes** *reels.*

Prince Khufurah   But not a common one among Klatchians, Ahmed. Incidentally, Commander, was that resplendent lady who introduced us your first wife?

Vimes   Er . . . she's all my wives. I mean . . .

Prince Khufurah   Could I offer you twenty camels for her?

Vimes   This is another test, isn't it?

Prince Khufurah   Well done, Sir Samuel. You're *good* at this. Do you know, Mr Boggis of the Thieves' Guild was prepared to accept fifteen?

Vimes   For Mrs Boggis? Nah . . . four camels, tops. Maybe four camels and a goat in a good light. And if she's had a shave.

Prince Khufurah   Very good. Very good. I am afraid, Commander, that some of *your* people feel that just because *my* people invented advanced mathematics and all-day camping that we are complete barbarians who'd try to buy their wives at the drop of, shall we say a turban? I'm surprised Unseen University is giving me an honorary degree, what with me being so backward.

Vimes   Oh? What degree is that?

Prince Khufurah   Apparently it's, er . . . *Doctorum Adamus cum Flabello Dulci.*

Vimes *snorts.*

Prince Khufurah   Sorry?

Vimes   Nothing, your highness.

Prince Khufurah   Well, if you will excuse me. I must have a word with the Archchancellor.

She moves off. **71-Hour Ahmed** *sidles up to* **Vimes**.

71-Hour Ahmed   If you change your mind, offendi, I give you twenty-five camels, no problem. May your loins be full of fruit.

He starts to leave, then turns and comes back to **Vimes**.

The Prince tells me that *Doctorus Adamus cum Flabello Dulci* means Doctor of Sweet Fanny Adams. A wizard wheeze, yes? Oh, how we are laughing.

Blackout.

Scene Six

A balcony overlooking the Convivium Parade.

Captain Carrot *and* **Corporal Angua** *are looking down on the parade. Noise, off, of crowd. As they speak, the procession enters, below them, at a slow pace.*

Angua He looks very smart, doesn't he?

Captain Carrot *looks.*

Angua Commander Vimes, I mean.

Carrot Oh, yes. I'm not sure that he enjoys looking smart, though. I know he was dreading walking at the head of the procession.

Angua What's that he's carrying?

Carrot The ceremonial truncheon. It has a silver plate engraved with 'Keeper of the King's Peace'. Sir Samuel thinks it's stupid. 'Even a constable gets a sword,' he said, 'What use is a truncheon supposed to be?' Oh no – what's he doing . . . ?

Angua He's trying door handles in the shops along the route. But why?

Carrot Oh no. He's drifted off.

Angua What?

Carrot He's back on the beat. He's forgotten where he is. Oh no, this could be really embarrassing. What's the procession doing?

Angua Following his every step. They probably think it's some form of tradition.

Carrot (*covering his eyes*) What's he doing now?

Angua He's, er, taking out the 'ceremonial' packet of cigars from his helmet. Oh . . . and he's lighting one. He's just blown a smoke ring.

Carrot The first of the day. He always does that . . .

Angua And he's tossing the truncheon up into the air and catching it . . . like he does with his sword when he's thinking . . . he looks quite happy.

Carrot He's tired, that's what it is. He's been running around overseeing things for days. You know what a hands-on person he is.

Angua Let's hope the Patrician lets him stay that way.

Carrot Oh, his lordship wouldn't . . . He wouldn't. Would he?

Angua He's stopped. He's dropped the truncheon . . . he's seen something! There! Look! On the top of the Barbican – there's someone there!

Carrot (*looking*) There shouldn't be anyone there. It's been sealed up for . . . oh, my gods, they have a crossbow!

Angua (*looking back at the street*) The Commander's running for the Barbican. He's got a whole parade of dignitaries following him!

Crowd noise. On stage, **Vimes** *runs on, across the stage and off the other side. He is followed, at a run, by a number of dignitaries including* **Lord Vetinari** *and the* **Prince Khufurah***, who stumbles halfway and falls to the ground. The dignitaries gather round him.*

Carrot Look!

Angua No! Prince Khufurah!

Carrot What?

Angua   He's been shot! Come on!

They rush off as the lights black out.

Scene Seven

Patrician's Palace.

On stage are **Vimes** *and* **Captain Carrot**.

Vimes   Let me see that again.

Captain Carrot *hands him a square of paper and a clove.*

Carrot   I can't see anything in that tourist's iconograph picture, Sir Samuel. What do you see?

Vimes   What they want me to, I suspect.

Carrot   Who's they?

Vimes   Dunno. One step at a time. You know what I always say.

Carrot   Yessir. 'Everyone's guilty of something, especially the one's that aren't.' Sir.

Vimes   No, not that one . . .

Carrot   Er, 'Always take into consideration the fact that you might be dead wrong,' sir?

Vimes   No . . .

Carrot   'How come Nobby ever got a job as a Watchman?' sir? You say that one a lot.

Vimes   No. I meant: 'Always act stupid,' Carrot.

Carrot   Ah right. From now on I shall recall that that's what you always say.

Lord Vetinari *glides in.*

Lord Vetinari   Ah, Vimes. Captain.

Vimes   Sir.

Lord Vetinari   Let us not beat about the bush, Commander. How did the man get up there when your, er, people had checked everywhere so thoroughly last night? Magic?

Vimes   We think someone got in where the windows were boarded up and pulled the boards back after him. The dust had been disturbed.

Lord Vetinari   The situation is grave, Vimes.

Vimes   Yes, sir?

Lord Vetinari   Prince Khufurah was seriously injured. And Prince Cadram, we understand, is beside himself with rage. You have identified the assassin?

Vimes   Yes. He is, was, called Ossie Brunt, sir. Did odd jobs from time to time. Bit of a loner. No relatives or friends that we can find.

Lord Vetinari   And that's all you fellows know?

Vimes   It took some time to identify him, sir.

Lord Vetinari   Oh, why should that be?

Vimes   Couldn't give you the technical answer, sir. But it looked to me as though he wouldn't have needed a coffin, sir. You could've posted him between two barn doors.

Lord Vetinari   Was he acting alone?

Vimes   We only found one body, sir, and a lot of fallen masonry. I've put my best people on the job.

Lord Vetinari   Really?

Vimes   Sergeant Colon and Corporal Nobbs, sir.

Lord Vetinari (*with a smile*)   Oh, right.

No reaction from **Vimes**.

Lord Vetinari   Oh, you're serious. (*He clears his throat genteelly.*) We are getting some very threatening noises, Commander.

Vimes   What can I say, sir? I saw someone in the tower, I ran, someone shot the Prince with a bow and arrow and then I found a man at the bottom of the tower, obviously dead, with a broken bow and a lot of rock beside him. The storm last night probably loosened things up. I can't make up facts that don't exist, sir.

Lord Vetinari   So, a lone bowman with a mad grudge. Well, thank you, Captain Carrot, I'm sure you have people to arrest.

Carrot   Sir.

He exits.

Lord Vetinari   Strange days, Commander. I gather that this afternoon Captain Carrot was on the roof of the Opera House firing arrows down towards the archery butts.

Vimes   Very keen lad, sir.

Lord Vetinari   It could well be that the distance from the Opera roof to the butts is about the same as, say, the distance from the roof of the Barbican to the spot where the Prince was shot.

Vimes   Really, sir?

Lord Vetinari   And why was he doing this?

Vimes   Did you know, sir, that there still is a law requiring adult citizens to do one hour's archery practice every day?

Lord Vetinari   Do you know why I just sent Captain Carrot away?

Vimes   Nossir.

Lord Vetinari   He is an honest young man. Did you know that he twitches whenever he hears you tell a direct lie?

Vimes   Really, sir?

Lord Vetinari   I can't stand to see his poor face twitch all the time.

Vimes   Very thoughtful of you, sir.

Lord Vetinari   Where was the second bowman, Vimes?

Vimes (*damn*) Second bowman, sir?

Lord Vetinari   Have you ever had a hankering to go on the stage, Vimes?

Vimes   No, sir.

Lord Vetinari   Pity. I'm certain you are a great loss to the acting profession. I believe you said the man had put the boards back after him?

Vimes   Yes, sir.

Lord Vetinari   *Nailed* them back?

Vimes   Yes, sir.

Lord Vetinari   From the *outside*?

Vimes   Yes, sir.

Lord Vetinari   A particularly resourceful *lone* bowman, then.

Pause.

Colon and Nobbs are investigating this? Really?

Vimes   Yes, sir.

Lord Vetinari   If I were to ask you why, you'd pretend not to understand?

Vimes   Sir?

Lord Vetinari (*into* **Vimes***'s ear, with a definite edge to his voice*) If you say 'sir' again in that stupid voice, Vimes, I swear there will be trouble.

Vimes   They're good men, sir.

Lord Vetinari   However, some people might consider them to be . . . unimaginative, solid and . . . how shall I put it? Possessed of an inbuilt ability to accept the first explanation that presents itself and then bunk off somewhere for a quiet smoke? A certain lack of imagination? An ability to get out of their depth on a wet pavement?

Vimes I hope you are not impugning my men, sir?

Lord Vetinari Vimes, Sergeant Colon and Corporal Nobbs have never *been* pugned in their entire lives.

Vimes Sir?

Lord Vetinari And yet . . . we do not need complications, Vimes. An ingenious lone madman . . . well, there are many madmen. A regrettable incident.

Vimes Yes, sir. Fred and Nobby don't like complications either, sir.

Lord Vetinari We need simple answers, Vimes.

Vimes Sir. Fred and Nobby are *good* at simple.

Lord Vetinari Ah. Simple men see the simple truth.

Vimes That is a fact, sir.

Lord Vetinari You are learning fast, Vimes. You may go.

As **Vimes** *reaches the door.*

Lord Vetinari Oh – one more thing, Vimes. What happens when they have found the simple truth?

Vimes Can't argue with the truth, sir.

Vimes *exits.*

Lord Vetinari (*to himself*) In my experience, Vimes, you can argue with anything.

Vetinari *turns and walks upstage. He presses a concealed button. A door slides open. He exits. Blackout. We hear footsteps along a stone flagged corridor, interrupted from time to time by unlocking creaky, heavy doors. The lights come up, very gloomy (green light?).* **Lord Vetinari** *enters downstage left, makes his way cautiously along the 'corridor' leading to another concealed button, which he presses. A wall slides open to reveal* **Leonard of Quirm**, *sitting at a table full of* *clutter, papers and pens/inks. Just as the door opens there is a bang and a puff of smoke.* **Leonard** *stands with a smoking, twisted piece of machinery in his hand.*

Leonard of Quirm   Oh dear.

Lord Vetinari   Ah, Leonard. What was that?

Leonard of Quirm (*coming out of his room and into the corridor*) An experimental device for turning chemical energy into rotary motion. The problem, you see, is getting the little black pellets of black powder into the combustion chamber at exactly the right speed and one at a time. If two ignite together – well, we have an *external* combustion engine.

Lord Vetinari   And what would be the purpose of it?

Leonard of Quirm   I believe it could replace the horse.

Lord Vetinari   One of the advantages of the horse that people often point out . . . is that it very seldom explodes. Almost never, in my experience. Except for that unfortunate occurrence in the hot summer three years ago. (*He picks up two furry dice from the table.*) And these?

Leonard of Quirm   I don't know why I thought they would make it go better. It was just an idea.

Lord Vetinari   Indeed.

He returns the dice and picks up a blueprint.

And this? It looks like a war machine.

Leonard of Quirm   Oh that. It's just a throwing arm for balls of molten sulphur. I calculate it could have a range of half a mile.

Lord Vetinari   Really? And it could be built?

Leonard of Quirm   In theory, yes. But no one would ever do it. Rain unquenchable fire down upon fellow humans? You'd never find an artisan to build such a terrible weapon, or a soldier who'd pull the lever — that's part 3(b) on the plan, by the way . . . next to that sketch for an underwater boat.

Lord Vetinari Ah yes. But I imagine these huge power arms could not work without breaking . . .

Leonard of Quirm Seasoned ash and yew, laminated and held together by special steel bolts.

Lord Vetinari You are truly an 'ideas' person, Leonard. A genius, some would say.

Leonard of Quirm Yes, my lord.

Lord Vetinari But not everyone has your simple humanity, Leonard. There are people who might take your brilliant thoughts – (*He picks up a drawing.*) such as this one – for a device that could destroy mountains – and use them for bad purposes. (*He pockets this particular plan during* **Leonard***'s next line.*)

Leonard of Quirm (*sadly*) I know, my Lord. It is good of you to protect me so well.

Lord Vetinari Indeed. Have I told you by the way that the Klatchian situation is worsening?

Leonard of Quirm Very clever people, the Klatchians. Alchemy, metalwork, chemistry . . .

Lord Vetinari Oh dear. But surely all that was some time ago . . .

Leonard of Quirm Indeed, they must have made considerable progress by now. In many areas, they wrote the scroll, you know.

Lord Vetinari Ah. Oh dear.

Leonard of Quirm Yes indeed. Do you know, I suspect that they could be quite dangerous, if they so chose.

Lord Vetinari (*glumly*) Indeed. Thank you. I think you're telling me more than I really wanted to know.

Leonard of Quirm But you said there was a problem with Klatch?

Lord Vetinari   Mmm? Oh. Yes. Have you heard of the lost kingdom of Leshp?

Leonard of Quirm   Oh yes, I did some sketches there a few years ago. Some interesting aspects and fauna.

Lord Vetinari   Well, it's just resurfaced in the Circle Sea and a dispute has arisen about its . . . you did what? You've *been* to Leshp?

Leonard of Quirm   Yes, my lord.

Lord Vetinari   Then, Leonard, we must talk. And quickly.

He puts an arm around **Leonard**'s *shoulder and leads him back to his 'cell' as the lights fade to blackout.*

To start with, how does this underwater boat thing of yours *work?*

Leonard of Quirm   The principle's very simple, my Lord. You see I simply started by observing the way in which the ramora fish clings on to the shark . . .

The lights have blacked out.

Scene Eight

The Watch House.

On stage is **Vimes**. **Corporal**s **Littlebottom** *and* **Angua**, *and* **Captain Carrot** *enter.*

Vimes   Ah, come in, all of you. Corporal Littlebottom. How did you get on?

Cheery Littlebottom   I've had a chance to look at the clove that you found at the scene of the assassin's death, Commander, and I have found teeth marks. Looks like someone was chewing it like a toothpick.

Vimes   In that case I would say that this was last touched by a man of swarthy complexion. About my height. (*Assuming* *your* **Ahmed** is *roughly* **Vimes**'s *height*.) Bearded. Scarred. Carrying a large sword.

Littlebottom *looks impressed.*

Vimes Detective work is like gambling. It helps if you know the winners in advance.

Littlebottom *exits.*

Vimes Now then, Angua?

Angua I followed that clove smell from the scene all the way to the docks. Then I lost it. Sorry. I was all right through the fish market and the slaughterhouse district. But when it went into the spice market . . .

Vimes Yes, of course. Not your fault. He's a clever man. And how did you get on, Captain?

Carrot I used the bow you found by the body of the alleged assassin, Commander. From the top of the Opera it was possible to hit the target in the butts, but . . .

Vimes But . . . you're a strong man, Captain. The late 'assassin' was very weedy.

Carrot The crossbow was a Burleigh and Stronginthearm 'Shureshott Five', sir. That has a hundred-pound draw. Our body couldn't have fired it, sir. Not with any accuracy.

Vimes As I thought. (*He draws out the picture again and looks at it.*) The Prince was shot in the chest by a man behind him who could not possibly have used the bow that he didn't shoot him with from the wrong direction.

Carrot And Constable Downspout found this, sir, (*Passes an arrow to* **Vimes**.) in the upper wall of a building along the route.

Vimes Where a misguided arrow fired by a small weak man pulling a heavy bow, with the bow wobbling all over the place . . .

Corporal Angua *takes the arrow and smells it.*

Angua Yes, sir. Ossie. Definitely.

Vimes Thank you, Corporal. Right – you, Carrot, and you, Angua . . . you're on the case.

Carrot But, sir, I thought that Fred and Nobby were investigating this?

Vimes Sergeant Colon and Corporal Nobbs are investigating why the late Ossie tried to kill the Prince. And do you know what? They're going to find lots of clues. I just know it.

Carrot But we know he couldn't . . .

Vimes Isn't this fun? But don't get in Colon's way, mm? And trust no one.

Carrot Er . . . I can trust Angua, can't I?

Vimes Well, yes, of course you . . .

Carrot And you, presumably.

Vimes Me, well, obviously. That goes without say –

Carrot Corporal Littlebottom? She can be very helpful . . .

Vimes Cheery? Yes, certainly you can.

Carrot Sergeant Detritus? I've always thought that he was pretty trustworthy . . .

Vimes Detritus? Oh yes, he . . .

Carrot Nobby, though. Should I . . . ?

Angua Carrot, I understand what he *means*. Come on.

Vimes I don't want written reports. This is . . . unofficial. But *officially* unofficial, if you see what I mean.

Carrot Sir, I . . .

Angua Yes, sir, we understand.

Vimes Listen to the streets. Have a quiet look at things. Get to the bottom of things. And trust no . . . Trust practically no one. All right? Except trustworthy people.

Lights out.

Scene Nine

Vimes's *house.*

Vimes *and* **Lady Ramkin** *are sitting at their table, eating.*
Vimes *has a spoon held half-way to his mouth.*

Vimes (*reading*) 'Also, we took the iconograph picture to
the man in the weapons shop and he said that it was the
diseased who bought the crossbow . . . '

Good grief. (*He turns back a page in the report.*) ' . . . also in
addition to the Klatchian money in the flat, you could tell
there was one of them there because of there was sand on
the floor . . . '

He'd still got sand on his sandals? After a five-hundred-mile
boat trip?

Lady Ramkin Sam? Your soup will be cold. You've had
that spoon poised like that for five minutes. What are you
reading?

Vimes Fred Colon's report of his and Nobby's investigations.
About the only things they haven't found are the bunch of
dates and the camel hidden under the pillow . . . Er, is
something wrong, dear?

Lady Ramkin Can you remember when we last had
dinner together, Sam?

Vimes Tuesday, wasn't it?

Lady Ramkin That was the Guild of Merchants' annual
dinner, Sam.

Vimes But you were there, too, weren't you?

Lady Ramkin And then you rushed off.

Vimes Policing's a twenty-four-hour job, my dear. There's
so much to do, Sybil.

Lady Ramkin You ought to delegate.

Vimes So I'm told. Well, let's have an evening in tonight then, dear. There's a blazing log fire in the withdrawing room.

Lady Ramkin No there isn't, Sam. I'm afraid the footman's gone off to be a bugler in the Duke of Eorle's regiment.

There is a knocking at the door.

Vimes Well, I'm sure that *I* can find the woodshed. I've lit enough fires in my time . . .

Corporals **Littlebottom** *and* **Angua** *rush in.*

Cheery Littlebottom Commander! Commander, you must come at once! It's murder, sir!

Vimes *looks at* **Lady Ramkin**. *She stands.*

Lady Ramkin Of course, dear.

She exits and leaves him to it.

Vimes Corporal?

Angua We went to the Unseen University, as you suggested, sir. A man had been standing by the window overlooking the parade. Long hair, a bit dry, stank of expensive shampoo. He was the man who nailed the boards back after Ossie got into the Barbican.

Vimes Are you sure?

Angua Is this nose ever wrong?

Vimes Sorry. Go on.

Angua I'd say he was a heavy-set man. A bit bulky for his height. He didn't wash a lot, but when he did he used Windpike's Soap, the cheap brand. But expensive shampoo, which is odd. Quite new boots. And a green coat.

Vimes You can smell the colour?

Angua The dye. I *think* he shot a bow. I could smell the wood of the stock and a trace of silk from the bowstring.

Vimes   How long was he there?

Angua   Two or three hours, I'd say. He didn't move around much. Or smoke. Or spit. He just stood and waited. A professional. Oh . . . and he had dandruff. Bad dandruff.

Vimes   Green coat and bad dandruff? That'll be Snowy Slopes. He's very good at killing people he's never met. Have you been to his rooms?

Cheery Littlebottom   Yes, sir. He'd been beheaded.

Angua (*holding out a clove*)   We found this, sir.

Vimes   A clove. And there was that one you found on the floor at Ossie's flat, too. That was better hidden than the other clues that Nobby and Fred found. Maybe that means it's a real clue. Anything else?

Angua   There was a fire at the Klatchian Embassy, sir. No-one was injured sir. A man (*describe* **71-Hour Ahmed**) was seen carrying people out of the building.

Vimes   Quite a night, so far. Anyone know what time it is?

Disorganiser   Bingly, Bingly, Beep!

Vimes   Oh no.

He takes out the **Disorganiser**.

Disorganiser   It is . . . about nine-ish.

Vimes   Nineish?

Disorganiser   Yep. Precisely . . . about nineish.

Vimes   Precisely about nineish??

Disorganiser   Yesterday you said if I didn't stop all that eight fifty-six and ten seconds stuff I would be looking at a hammer from below. And when I pointed out, Mr Insert-Name-Here, that this would invalidate my warranty, you said I could take my warranty and . . .

Angua   I thought you'd lost that thing, sir.

Disorganiser   Hah! Lost! I don't call putting me into a pair of trousers that were just going to the wash 'lost'.

Vimes   That was an accident.

Disorganiser   Oh? And dropping me in the dragon's feeding bowl? That was an accident, too, mm? Anyway, do you want your appointments for this evening?

Vimes   Do tell.

Disorganiser   You haven't any. You haven't told me any.

Vimes   There you are. Why should I have to tell *you*? Why can't *you* just tell *me* what's going to happen? That would be useful! If you were any good, that'd be your job.

Disorganiser   Do you know, he uses my instruction manual as a sort of diary so his wife won't know he doesn't know how to use me.

Vimes   And what about the Vimes manual? You've never bothered to find out how to use me!

Disorganiser   Humans come with a manual?

Vimes   It's be a good idea.

Angua   True.

Vimes   It could say things like – 'My owner keeps dropping me in the privvy. What am I doing wrong?' (*Closing the* **Disorganiser**.) But what does it all add up to, Corporal? The man we know didn't shoot the Prince is dead. The man who probably did . . . is also dead. Someone tried very clumsily to make it look like Ossie was paid by the Klatchians. OK, I can see why they'd want to do that. Politics. They get Snowy to do the real business and he helps poor dumb Ossie to take the fall and when the Watch prove that the Klatchians paid for it then that's another reason for fighting. And Snowy just slopes off. Only someone cured his dandruff for him.

Disorganiser   Bingly, Bingly, Beep.

Vimes (*opening it*) Oh hell. I don't want to know I haven't got any appointments!

Disorganiser You have one at ten p.m. The Rats' Chamber at the Palace.

Vimes Don't be stupid.

Disorganiser Please yourself.

Vimes And shut up.

Disorganiser I was just trying to help.

Vimes Where was I?

Angua Snowy Slopes, sir.

Vimes Ah yes. Now someone beheaded him. No doubt about it. And Snowy had tried to shoot the Prince. And so had Ossie.

Angua But Ossie only *thought* he was an assassin.

Vimes Yes, but if it had all gone to plan he *would* have thought he *was* the assassin. And then this convenient fire at the Embassy. Civil riot? Or a convenient way of smuggling someone out of the building in all the confusion? I wish we knew more about Klatch.

Colon Know the enemy, eh, sir?

Lieutenant Hornett *enters.*

Vimes Oh, I know the enemy, all right. It's Klatch I want to know more about.

Hornett Commander Vimes?

Vimes You're one of Rust's men, aren't you?

Hornett Lieutenant Hornett, sir. Er . . . his lordship has sent me to ask if you and your senior officers would be so good as to come to the palace at your convenience, sir.

Disorganiser Bingly, Bingly, Beep!

Vimes (*opening the* **Disorganiser**) Really? Were those his exact words?

Hornett In fact, sir, he said: 'Get Vimes and his mob up here right now.' Sir.

Disorganiser The time is ten p.m. precisely!

Blackout.

Scene Ten

The Patrician's Palace.

Lord Rust *is on stage.* **Lieutenant Hornett**, **Vimes**, **Captain Carrot**, **Corporal Angua** *and* **Sergeant**s **Colon** *and* **Detritus** *enter*

Rust Ah, Vimes.

Vimes Lord Vetinari on his holidays, is he?

Rust Lord Vetinari stepped down this evening, Vimes. Just for the duration of the emergency.

Vimes Really?

Rust Yes. He anticipated a certain . . . cynicism on your part, Commander, so he asked me to give you this letter.

He hands it over.

Vimes I see. You wanted me?

Rust Commander Vimes, I must ask you take into custody all the Klatchians in the city.

Vimes On what charge, sir?

Rust Commander, we are on the verge of a *war* with Klatch. Surely you understand?

Vimes No, sir.

Rust I'm talking about sabotage, spying. The city must be placed under martial law.

Vimes   And what sort of law's that, sir? Is it the one where you shout 'Stop!' *before* you fire, or the other kind. Sir.

Rust   It pleased you to be smart with Lord Vetinari, and for some reason he indulged you. I, on the other hand, know your type. You seem to feel that the law is some kind of big, glowing light in the sky which is not subject to control. And you are wrong. The law is what we tell it to be. I'm not going to add 'Do you understand?' because I *know* you understand and I am not going to try to reason with you.

Vimes   Oh?

Rust   Commander Vimes, the last few days point to a succession of judgemental errors on your part. The Prince Khufurah was shot, and you seemed helpless to prevent this or to find the criminal responsible.

Vimes   Sir?

Rust   And now Prince Khufurah has been kidnapped, Vimes. I don't know what's happened to the Prince and you seem to be making things worse. I am relieving you of command. The Watch will come under the direct control of this council. We duly appoint Captain Carrot as acting commander of the Watch.

Carrot   Sir! No, sir!

Rust   Very loyal. Very well, then . . . Sergeant Colon!

Colon   Nossir!

Rust   No?

Colon   You can put it where the sun doesn't shine. Sir!

Rust   I see. Sergeant Detritus . . .

Sergeant Detritus *shakes his head.*

Rust   No? Very well. I see the way this is going. Who is the most senior corporal, Mr Vimes?

Vimes (*with a smirk*)   Corporal Nobbs.

Rust Ah.

Vimes This is ridiculous.

He hands **Lord Rust** *his badge.*

Rust I see. You would rather be a civilian, mm?

Vimes A watchman *is* a civilian, you inbred streak of piss!

Rust *(after a pause)* Very well. Anyone else have empty gestures to make?

Sergeants **Colon** *and* **Detritus** *and* **Captain Carrot** *hand over their badges.*

Rust You too, Captain? I would have thought that you at least . . .

The **Klatchian Ambassador** *rushes in with two* **Klatchian Guards**.

Rust Ambassador? Your arrival is unannounced but . . .

Ambassador I have grave news, Lord Rust. There have been developments in the new land. Regrettable incidents. There and indeed here, in Ankh-Morpork. Reports are confused. Lord Rust, I must tell you that technically we are at war.

Vimes Technically?

Ambassador I must tell you that you are being given twelve hours to remove all your citizens from Leshp. If that is done, all matters will be satisfactorily resolved, for the time being.

Rust It is unfortunate that things have come to this. I am obliged to send a similar message in relation to your people on Leshp. With similar timescales.

Vimes What? You can't just start a war like this. What about diplomacy?

Rust War, Vimes, is a continuation of diplomacy by other means. As you would know, were you *really* a gentleman.

But, as you have been at pains to point out, you are a civilian. You have no place here.

Vimes *turns on his heel and storms out. The rest of the* **Watch** *follow as the lights black out.*

Scene Eleven

Vimes's *house.*

Vimes *and* **Lady Ramkin** *are on stage, with the* **Disorganiser**. *There is a crowd noise offstage.*

Disorganiser   Bingly, Bingly, Beep! Good morning, Insert Name Here. The time is one o'clock PM, precisely.

Vimes   Wha . . . ? Will you stop doing that!

Lady Ramkin   Sam?

Vimes   Yes, dear.

Lady Ramkin   Why are your men outside recruiting for 'Vimes First of Foot'? Are you forming your own regiment?

Vimes   Did I really call Lord Rust a long streak of . . . ?

Lady Ramkin   Yes, Sam, you did. Fred Colon told me. I went out with Ronnie Rust once. Bit of a cold fish. I'd say you got it just about right. But Sam, what about your men . . .

Vimes *(taking out* **Vetinari**'s *letter)*   'Sir Samuel Vimes, Knight.' And then a blank sheet of paper. What do you think he meant by that?

Lady Ramkin   I don't know, Sam. Is that why you've been looking through the chivalry books in our library?

Lord Rust *bursts on.*

Rust   Vimes? Sorry, Sybil – had to let myself in. What's happened to your butler?

Lady Ramkin   Hello, Ronnie. Joined up, I'm afraid.

Rust   Hrrm. Now Vimes. What in hell's name is going on outside? What are you doing? You've been relieved of command. Why are you recruiting for the Watch?

Vimes   I'm not. I'm forming my own regiment.

Rust   You can't do that!

Vimes   Oh, I rather think I can. Lord Vetinari reminded me of the fact. *Sir* Samuel Vimes, Knight. (*He pulls out some detailed notes.*) Here, my lord. It's all here, in case you have any doubt. (*Reading.*) A lot of it is pretty damn stupid stuff, but *one* of them says in times of need a knight *has* to raise and maintain – you'll laugh when I tell you this – a body of armed soldiers! No one could have been more surprised than me, I don't mind telling you! Seemed like there was nothing for it but to go out and get myself some chaps together. Of course, most of the Watch have joined . . .

Rust   This is nonsense. And you, Vimes, are certainly no knight. Only a king can make . . .

Vimes   Oh, there're quite a few lordships created by the Patricians. Your friend Lord Downey, for one.

Rust   Very well, but before a knight is created he must spend a night's vigil watching his armour . . .

Vimes   Practically every night of my life. Any man who doesn't keep his eye on his armour round here, that man's got no armour in the morning.

Rust   . . . in prayer . . .

Vimes   That's me. Not a night goes past that I don't think 'Ye Gods, I hope I get through this alive.'

Rust   . . . and he must have proved himself on the field of combat. Against other trained men, Vimes. Not thieves and hooligans.

Vimes   Well, this probably isn't the best time, my lord, but if someone'll hold your coat I can spare you five minutes.

Rust   I know what you're doing, Vimes. In any case, you've had no formal training in arms.

Vimes You're right. Not how you mean, anyway. But I reckon I could take you on without breaking into a sweat.

Rust Very well, then. But your regiment will come under my command . . .

Vimes Strangely, no. Under the command of the king or his duly appointed representative. And there's been no appointed representative since some bastard cut off the last king's head . . .

Rust Your ancestor.

Vimes Oh yes, you're right. But *somebody* wanted this war. *Someone* paid to have Ossie Brunt and Snowy Slopes killed. *Someone* wanted the Prince dead. This isn't a war. This is a *crime*.

Anyway, I'd better not keep you from your warmongering, had I? Got such a lot of things to do. You know how it is. I have the swatches for the new uniforms in my office. It's so important to look right on the battlefield, don't you think?

Lord Rust *turns and walks out. Blackout.*

Scene Twelve

A wharf on the banks of the Ankh.

Captain Carrot, **Corporal**s **Angua** and **Nobbs** and **Sergeant Colon** *are on stage, looking out at the river.*

Colon A war'd do this place good. Everything's gone to pot these days.

Nobby Not like when we was kids, eh, Sarge?

Colon People trusted one another, Nobby.

Nobby People didn't have to lock their doors at night.

Colon S'right.

Nobby *Couldn't* lock them, in fact. Cos the buggers used to nick the locks as well.

Colon   Yeah, but at least they was nicking each *other's* stuff. Neighbourly-like. It's not as though they was *foreigners*.

Nobby   You ever met a Klatchian, Sarge? I mean a real one, you know, in the wild, like.

Colon   Well, no. But you know what? They're allowed three wives. That's criminal, that is.

Nobby   Yeah, cos here's me and I ain't even got one.

Colon   They eat funny grub. Curry and that.

Nobby   Like we do? When we're on late duty?

Colon   You tryin' to get me going? You *know* we're better'n Klatchians. Sayin' otherwise is treachery.

71-Hour Ahmed *crosses the stage. He is with, and supporting, an unidentifiable figure (***Prince Khufurah***) in a hooded, ground-length robe.*

71-Hour Ahmed   Ah, gentlemen and . . . heh, er, *lady*. Good day to you, offendis. Pardon me if I don't stay to chat, but I, er, *we* have a tide to catch.

They exit.

Colon   See? That's just what I mean . . .

Angua   Wait! That smell . . .

Carrot   What, from Mr Ahmed, you mean?

Angua   Yes. It was . . . cloves. Cloves.

Carrot   Like we found in Snowy Slopes's room?

Angua   Yes. And 71-Hour Ahmed also has a large sharp sword that could sever a head very easily.

Carrot   Right, then, in that case . . .

Angua   No. You can't go onto their ship. There're armed men. What will they think when they see an armed soldier running towards their ship?

Carrot   But I'm not a soldier.

Angua Will that bother them?

Carrot I can't just let him get away. He's a suspect.

Angua With diplomatic immunity. But look there – they have hunting dogs on the ship . . .

Carrot No, Angua, I can't let you . . .

Angua I can get on – in wolf form – without being detected. I would be able to listen in, to see what he was about. Don't worry.

Strobe. Music. **Corporal Angua** *starts to change as she lopes off.*

Carrot Angua! You men, wait here. I'm going to follow – discreetly – and make sure she's safe.

Pause.

Nobby Would you fight them, then, Fred?

Colon I s'pose as an hexperienced military man, I'd have to.

Nobby You'd join up, would you? Go to the front?

Colon Werl, my fortay lies in training, so I'd be better staying here and training up new recruits.

Nobby At the back, as it were.

Colon Now look here, Corporal Nobbs . . .

Leonard of Quirm *enters.*

Leonard of Quirm Am I by any chance addressing the heroic Sergeant Colon and the . . . er, *the* Corporal Nobbs?

Colon That is us, citizen.

Leonard of Quirm Ah good. I was very specifically told to come and find you. By any means necessary.

Nobby Bribery would be good.

Colon *Who* told you?

Leonard of Quirm Lord Vetinari.

Nobby The Patrician wants *us?*

Leonard of Quirm Yes, he said you had special qualities.

Colon Right. And will we have to work under cover again?

Leonard of Quirm Er, there will be a strong element of *under*, yes.

Colon (*to* **Nobby**) Under cover means not getting stabbed and shot at, right? And what's the most important thing a professional soldier wants not to happen to him?

Nobby Not gettin' stabbed and shot!

Leonard of Quirm Good. Tell me, Sergeant, are you of a nautical persuasion?

Colon Nossir. Happily married man, sir.

Leonard of Quirm I meant, have you ploughed the ocean waves at all?

Colon Can't catch me that way, sir. Everyone knows the horses would sink.

Leonard of Quirm What? Oh. Right. (*He tries one last time.*) Have you, in the past, floated around on the sea, in a boat, as it were?

Colon Me sir? Not me, sir. It's the sight of the waves going up and down, sir.

Leonard of Quirm Really? Well, happily seeing the waves will *not* be a problem.

Blackout.

Scene Thirteen

A room at the Watch House.

Vimes *is alone on stage, writing in a book. We hear his thoughts over the speakers, as he writes.*

Vimes (*voice-over*) Assembling facts. That's what it's all about. Someone wanted the Watch to say that the assassination was inspired by Klatch. But who? Someone had beheaded Snowy Slopes where he stood and left him deader than six buckets of fish-bait. And 71-Hour Ahmed has a very sharp sword. Let's say he was the Prince's bodyguard and that he'd found out . . .

But who'd tell him? And if he knew Slopes was the assassin, maybe he also knew who'd *paid* Slopes.

Disorganiser Bingly, Bingly, Beep.

Vimes What is it now?

Disorganiser Three-oh-five p.m. Interview with Corporal Littlebottom re missing Sergeant Colon.

Vimes I never arranged anything like that. Who told you . . . ? Are you telling me I've got an appointment and don't even know about it?

Disorganiser That's right.

Vimes So how do *you* know about it? You can tell me about appointments I don't know about?

Disorganiser Look, you can have an appointment at any time, right? So therefore *any* appointment exists *in potentia* . . .

Vimes What's that?

Disorganiser I merely select the most likely appointments from the known space-time matrix.

Vimes You're making this up. If it were true, then any second now . . .

There is a knock at the door. **Corporal Littlebottom** *enters.*

Cheery Littlebottom Sir! I was asked to give you this note, sir.

We hear **Sergeant Colon**'s *voice over the speakers as* **Vimes** *reads the note.*

Colon (*voice over*)   Have volunteered for a mission of Vital Importance. Nobby is here also. There will be statues of us when this is all over.

Vimes   Thank you, Corporal.

Corporal Littlebottom *exits.*

Vimes   Pure coincidence.

Disorganiser   Right then. Bingly, Bingly, Beep. Three fifteen p.m. Emergency meeting with Captain Carrot about Corporal Angua.

A knock at the door.

Vimes (*with a resigned sigh*)   Come in, Captain.

Disorganiser   Hah!

Captain Carrot *enters, hurriedly.*

Vimes   Something's happened to Angua?

Carrot   How did you know?

Vimes   Let's just call it . . . intuition. I'm right, am I?

Carrot   Yes. She followed 71-Hour Ahmed onto a Klatchian ship, but now it's sailing and she's still on board!

Vimes   What the hell did she go *on* for?

Carrot   It was Ahmed. He was going to get away. And he looked like he was taking someone with him, sir.

Vimes   Who?

Carrot   Don't know, sir. They were all wrapped up, but they didn't look well. I watched at the dockside, sir. I think Ahmed knew that Angua wasn't a real Klatchian hound.

Vimes   Carrot, there are people who, if their girlfriend was spirited away on a foreign ship, would dive into the Ankh – or at least run briskly over its crust – leap aboard and deal out merry hell. That might be the dumb thing to do but they'd do it. The *right* thing to do would be to seek help, but . . .

Carrot Personal isn't the same as important, sir.

Vimes I know, but . . . (*He sighs.*) Carrot, you are a strange man at times. Logical, rational, but strange. The city's gone mad, Carrot. We have a duty to stay here and fight if we have to. But we're also Watchmen and we have a responsibility to solve crime. I'm damned if I'll let our prime suspect kidnap one of my best officers and run back to Klatch. Fast boat, was it?

Carrot Yes, but it looked pretty heavy in the water.

Vimes Right. Well, Captain Jenkins owes us a big favour. Let's just go and call it in, eh?

Carrot Yes SIR!

Vimes *picks up his* **Disorganiser**. *He pauses for a moment as he weighs the options to stay or to go. They exit.*

Blackout.

Scene Fourteen

In the submarine dock.

Sergeant Colon, Corporal Nobbs *and* **Leonard of Quirm** *are on stage, looking at the submarine (fourth wall). Water effect.*

Colon Looks like a giant fish to me. Made of tin.

Nobby It'll never float. I can see where you've gone wrong there. Metal won't float. Everyone knows metal sinks.

Leonard of Quirm Not entirely true. In any case, this boat is designed to sink.

Colon What?

Leonard of Quirm Well, to travel underwater, anyway. Propulsion was a major headache, I'm afraid. I thought of paddles, and oars and even some kind of screw. Finally settled on that spinning fan thingie at the back. The linkage rods are a bit complicated and the pedalling will be a bit tiresome but the three of us should be able to get quite a turn of speed.

Nobby   What? Pedalling? *Under* water?

Leonard of Quirm   Yes, it'll be fun . . .

Nobby   But what about that screw whatsit on its sharp end?

Lord Vetinari *enters.*

Lord Vetinari   Ah, gentlemen. Leonard has explained everything to you?

Colon   You can't ask us to go into that thing, my lord! It will be suicide!

Lord Vetinari   No. No, I think you are wrong. I think that, in all probability, going into that thing will be a valiant and rewarding deed. I would venture to suggest that, in fact, it is *not* going into that thing that would be suicidal. I would welcome your views.

Colon   Ready to go, *sah*!

Lord Vetinari   Splendid.

Leonard of Quirm   I think we should all get in. I've lit the candle that'll burn down and sever the string that'll release the weights that'll pull the blocks out.

Colon   Er . . . what exactly is this thing called, Mr Da Quirm?

Leonard of Quirm   Well, because it is *submerged* in a *marine* environment, I've always called it the 'Going-Under-the-Water-Safely Device'. But usually I just think of it as . . . The Boat.

Nobby   Mr Leonard, where're we going?

Leonard of Quirm   His lordship wishes to go to Leshp.

Nobby   I thought as much. I thought: where don't I want to go? And there it is. Leshp. But if we have to pedal all the way, my knees will give out.

Leonard of Quirm   Oh my word, we won't have to *pedal* all the way. What did you think that big augur on the nose was for?

Nobby   Well, you could use it to drill into the hulls of enemy ships to sink them.

Leonard of Quirm   What? Use the Boat to sink ships? Sink ships with people on them? That would be inhuman! The augur is so we can attach ourselves to the bottoms of other ships so we can be carried along on their sail power.

Nobby   Oh. Clever.

Lord Vetinari   Carry on, Sergeant.

Lights black out as the scene ends.

Scene Fifteen

A room in Prince Cadram's Palace, Al Khali.

Prince Cadram, *a* **Mystic** *and* **General Ashal** *are on stage. They are peering into a crystal ball.*

General Ahsal   Well, tell the Prince Cadram what you see, mystic.

Prince Cadram   Thank you General Ashal, I can speak for myself. Well, what *can* you see?

Mystic   I see a boat, your highness.

Prince Cadram   A boat? *One* boat? They are sending only one boat?

Mystic   So it would appear, your highness.

General Ahsal   Our own military scryers have also been looking, highness. We do believe one of the men on the boat to be Vimes, sire.

Prince Cadram   Ah. The *useful* Commander Vimes.

General Ahsal   Indeed. And there has been a lot of activity all along the docks in Ankh-Morpork. Lord Rust seems to be setting off in pursuit of Commander Vimes. Following his lead, you might say. We have to take the view that the expeditionary force is setting out.

Prince Cadram   I thought we had at least a week, Ashal.

General Ahsal   Something must have happened, highness.

Prince Cadram   Oh well. Let us follow where fate points the way. You can put *your* fleet on standby, Ashal. We do not need to go to them, now. *They* are coming to *us*. Where will they attack?

General Ahsal   Gebra, highness.

Prince Cadram   Gebra? Surely not. Our most heavily fortified city? Only an idiot would do that.

General Ahsal   I have studied Lord Rust in some depth, highness. Remember, he doesn't expect us to fight, so the size of our forces doesn't really worry him.

Prince Cadram (*not very sincerely*)   Any news of my poor brother, Khufurah?

General Ahsal (*equally insincere*)   Alas, no, highness.

Prince Cadram   Our agents must search harder. The world is watching.

General Ahsal   Correct, highness.

Mystic   I could have a look in the crystal ball, sire . . . ?

Prince Cadram   Silence, mystic!

Blackout.

Act Two

Scene One

On board the submarine.

Various dials and levers. Four small seats, three with pedal attachments. Pinging noise. **Vetinari**, **Leonard of Quirm**, **Sergeant Colon** *and* **Corporal Nobbs** *are on stage.* **Lord Vetinari** *is holding a handkerchief over his nose (against the smells emrging from* **Nobby***) and is reading a copy of* The Hunt for Red Sektober. **Nobby** *and* **Colon** *are pedalling furiously, powering the submarine's propeller.* **Colon** *is wafting a bit of card at* **Nobby**.

Nobby   Lay off, Sarge – you can hardly smell it now. Sarge?

Colon   Yes, Nobby?

Nobby   Tell me again about our special qualities.

Colon   Shut up and keep pedalling, Nobby.

Nobby   Right, Sarge.

Pause.

It's like being inside a sewing machine, this is. How long we bin going?

He turns and looks at **Vetinari**, *who takes the handkerchief from his nose and speaks without looking up.*

Lord Vetinari   Carry on, Corporal.

Leonard of Quirm   My lord, when we surfaced ten minutes ago to, er . . . to, er . . . to allow Corporal Nobbs to clear the air, I spotted another ship on the same course as us. I have now steered us underneath it and I will extend the augur and attach us, in the manner of the ramora fish, to the underside of their vessel.

Lord Vetinari   Excellent. I am sure that these two gentlemen will welcome the rest.

Lights cross-fade to the Klatchian vessel, above them. Water noise. Seagulls, etc. **Corporal Angua** *is on stage, wearing a large silver collar and chain.* **71-Hour Ahmed** *enters.*

71-Hour Ahmed   Ah, Miss Angua. I see you have elected to return to human form again. I trust the food has been to your liking?

Angua   Even in animal form, Ahmed, it was almost uneatable. (*Threateningly.*) And a werewolf, may I remind you, will eat virtually anything.

71-Hour Ahmed   Indeed. That is why I have taken the precaution of securing you with a *silver* collar and chain.

Angua   How did you know it was me? When I came onto the boat?

71-Hour Ahmed   Oh, Miss Angua. Do not take me for a fool. Noble as Klatchian hunting dogs are, none of them have the innate breeding of a member of the ruling family of Überwald. Delphine Angua von Überwald, mm? With you on board, Commander Vimes is sure to pursue me.

The look-out rushes on.

Look-Out   Sir, sir! A terrible thing, sir!

71-Hour Ahmed   What. Speak up, man.

Look-Out   Just now, sir! Behind us! A giant monster rose from the waves!

71-Hour Ahmed   Who knows what lies on the floor of the sea?

Look-Out   And its breath, sir. It was like the stench of a thousand privvies! And then it spoke!

71-Hour Ahmed   Indeed? What did it say?

Look-Out   I did not understand it, sir. I am a simple man. But it sounded like – 'Ye gods, that was better out than in, Sarge.'

71-Hour Ahmed   And what did that mean to you?

Look-Out Nothing, sir.

71-Hour Ahmed You have not spent much time in Ankh-Morpork?

Look-Out No, sir.

71-Hour Ahmed Return to your post.

The look-out exits.

And we seem to have lost some speed. I do not believe in sea monsters, Miss Angua, but no matter. I see on the horizon that we seem to be being followed by another vessel, too. That will be Vimes. But it isn't gaining on us. We are too fast for him. I don't want us to lose him.

He walks off.

Angua Carrot. It's *you* in that ship isn't it? I can sense it. But down there . . . ? Only Nobby can foul the air like that. But how are he and Fred Colon travelling *under* our ship . . . ?

Lights cross-fade to the submarine. They are playing Scrabble.

Colon Er . . . if I add this A and this O and this I and this D, then I can use that V to make 'avoid', and that gets me . . . what's that blue square, Len?

Leonard of Quirm A 'Three Times Ye Value of Ye Letter' score.

Lord Vetinari Well done, Sergeant. I do believe that puts you in the lead.

Colon (*clearing his throat nervously*) Er . . . I do believe it does, my lord.

Lord Vetinari However – I find that you have left me the use of my U, N and A, B, L, E which incidentally lands me on this 'Three Times Ye Whole Word' square and, I rather suspect, wins me the game.

Sergeant Colon *sighs with relief.*

Lord Vetinari A capital game, Leonard. What did you say it was called?

Leonard of Quirm   I call it my 'Make Words With Letters That Have All Been Mixed Up Game', my lord.

Lord Vetinari   Ah. Yes. Obviously. Well done.

Nobby   Huh. An' I got three points. They was perfectly good words, too.

Leonard of Quirm   Strange. We seem to have stopped moving. Let me open the listening tube to the surface.

Noise of muffled Klatchian voices.

Colon   Heathen Klatchian talk. What're they gabbling about?

Lord Vetinari   'What nephew of a camel cut the rigging?'

Leonard of Quirm (*now looking into a periscope*)   There's another ship following us. I can see its bow light.

Lord Vetinari   Where are we, Leonard?

Leonard of Quirm   Well, my star charts are out of date, of course, but if you would care to wait until the sun rises, I've invented a device for ascertaining our position by reference to the sun . . .

Lord Vetinari   Where are we *now*, Leonard?

Leonard of Quirm   Er . . . in the middle of the Circle Sea, I suspect.

Lord Vetinari   Then Leshp should be in this vicinity?

Leonard of Quirm   Well, yes.

Lord Vetinari   Good. With no rigging, the ship above us is going nowhere. Unhitch us so we can peddle ashore under cover of darkness.

Leonard of Quirm   My lord, what about the ship following us?

Lord Vetinari   Mm? Oh, that will be Vimes.

Lights cross-fade to **Vimes***'s ship. Sea noise, seagulls, etc. Onstage are* **Vimes** *and* **Captain***s* **Carrot** *and* **Jenkins**.

Vimes Are we gaining on them?

Captain Jenkins We might be. There's a lot of sea between us.

Carrot All the lads are bedded down, sir.

Vimes Right.

Carrot I'll turn in too, for a couple of hours, if it's all right with you, sir.

Vimes Sorry. Captain?

Carrot I'll get my head down.

Vimes But . . . but . . . we're in hot pursuit of your girlfriend, among other things.

Carrot Yes, sir.

Vimes So aren't you . . . you mean you can . . . you want to . . . you want to go for a bit of a *nap*?

Carrot To be fresh when we catch up with them, yes, sir.

Vimes You'll be able to *get* to sleep, will you?

Carrot Oh, yes. I owe it to Angua.

Vimes Oh. Well, goodnight, then.

Captain Carrot *exits*.

Captain Jenkins Is he for real?

Vimes Yes.

Captain Jenkins I mean . . . would *you* go for a snooze if we was chasing *your* girl? Mind you, if it was Lady Sybil, their ship'd be a bit lower in the water!

Vimes You just watch . . . the sea.

Voice (*off*) They're slowing down, skipper!

Vimes What'd he say?

Captain Jenkins They're slowing down. What'll you do when we catch them?

Vimes Er . . . we'll swing across to their ship with cutlasses in our teeth?

Captain Jenkins Really? I've only ever seen that done once. Years ago.

Vimes Oh yes?

Captain Jenkins Yes, this lad had seen the idea in a book, and he swung across onto the other ship's rigging with his cutlass clenched, as you say, between his teeth.

Vimes Yes?

Captain Jenkins 'Topless Harry' we wrote on his coffin.

Disorganiser Bingly, Bingly, Beep!

Vimes (*taking out the* **Disorganiser**) Good grief, what now?

Disorganiser Eight p.m. Narrowly escape assassination by Klatchian Spy.

Vimes Where?

Disorganiser Corner of Brewer Street and Broad Way.

Vimes But I'm not there!

Disorganiser But you said you wanted to know what you *ought* to be doing!

Vimes Listen! No one has an appointment to be assassinated!

Disorganiser It's not my fault that I'm still set for the wrong time-line.

Vimes What does that mean?

Disorganiser I *thought* you hadn't read the manual. It says quite clearly that you should stick to one reality. Otherwise . . .

Vimes You mean, if I'd stayed in Ankh-Morpork I would have just escaped assassination?

Disorganiser Well done. Got there in the end!

Lights down. Sea noises. Lights up – we are now on the Klatchian ship again. **71-Hour Ahmed** *is on stage with* **Prince Khufurah**.

71-Hour Ahmed   Finally, highness. Finally, they are catching up. Captain!

The **Captain** *enters, carrying a piece of severed rope.*

Klatchian Captain   Sir, someone cut the ropes! Without wind, the boat can't move!

71-Hour Ahmed   Who would do that?

Klatchian Captain   I do not know, but . . .

71-Hour Ahmed   The infidel dogs are almost upon us! Your men will work faster!

Klatchian Captain   But who could have done such a thing? You were here, sir, and . . .

His eyes flick from the cut rope to **Ahmed***'s sword*

71-Hour Ahmed   Was there something you wished to say?

Klatchian Captain   Er . . . get that sail up right now, you festering sons of bitches!

He exits. There is a scream offstage. **Corporal Angua** *runs on.*

71-Hour Ahmed   Well, well. Miss Angua?

Angua   Prince Khufurah?

Prince Khufurah   How do you do, Corporal.

Angua   Excuse me.

She runs off. Splash. The **Klatchian Captain** *runs on.*

Klatchian Captain   Sir, I . . . the prisoner, sir. She escaped. We heard a splash. We think she jumped overboard, sir.

71-Hour Ahmed   Really?

He looks after **Corporal Angua**.

I can see no trace, Captain. She must have drowned. Back to your work, Captain.

Klatchian Captain   Yes, sir.

He exits.

Prince Khufurah   Ahmed?

71-Hour Ahmed   Trust me, my prince.

Scene shifts to the submarine. **Corporal Nobbs** *and* **Sergeant Colon** *are pedalling.* **Vetinari** *and* **Leonard of Quirm** *are peering out of the portholes.*

Colon   What're they looking for?

Nobby   Old Len keeps talking about hieroglyphs. What're they, Sarge?

Colon ⹁ Type of mollusc.

Nobby   Cor, you know everything, Sarge. So if we go much lower, will they be loweraglyphs?

Leonard of Quirm   Did you notice those fine strands of Dropley's Etiolated Bladderwrack? A marvellous growth which, as you'll know, is significant.

Lord Vetinari   Could we just assume for the moment that I have neglected my seaweed studies in recent years?

Leonard of Quirm   Really? Well, the loss is entirely yours. The point *is*, of course, that the Etiolated Bladderwrack is never usually found growing above thirty fathoms and it's only ten here.

Lord Vetinari   Ah. And the hieroglyphs. An alphabet of shapes and colours. Intriguing.

Colon   I know something about seaweed, sir.

Lord Vetinari   Yes, Sergeant?

Colon   Yessir. If it's wet, sir, it means it's going to rain.

Lord Vetinari Well done, Sergeant. I think it is quite possible that I will never forget you said that.

Nobby What're we doing down here, Sarge? Poking around. Looking at weird marks on rocks. And it smells funny.

Colon Well . . . if you'd lay off the beans . . .

Nobby No, *sulphur*, I mean.

Lord Vetinari One last little venture, gentlemen and then we can surface. Very well, Leonard, take us under.

Colon Er . . . aren't we underneath already, sir?

Lord Vetinari Only underneath the sea, Sergeant.

Colon Er . . .

Lord Vetinari Now we're going underneath the land.

Lights change back to **Vimes**'s *boat*. **Vimes** *and* **Captain**s **Carrot** *and* **Jenkins** *are onstage.*

Vimes We'll get her back, don't worry.

Carrot I'm not worried, sir. I'm *concerned*, of course.

Vimes Er . . . right. Erm, the men all right?

Carrot Yes, sir, but a word or two from you would help.

Sergeant Detritus, Corporal Littlebottom *and* **Constable Shoe** *enter.*

Vimes I don't pretend this is going to be easy, er . . . um, er, men. But our mission is to catch up with Angua and this bastard Ahmed and shake the truth out of him. Unfortunately this means following him into his own country. But we shouldn't let the prospect of being tortured to death dismay us, eh?

Carrot Fortune favours the brave, sir.

Vimes Good, good. Pleased to hear it, Captain. And what is fortune's position *vis à vis* heavily armed, well-prepared and excessively manned armies?

Carrot   Oh, no one's ever heard of Fortune favouring them, sir.

Detritus   I'm going to get really thick. Wiv de heat.

Cheery Littlebottom   Why's that?

Carrot   He's a troll, you see, Cheery, and they live in cold mountainous regions. Their brains work best at low temperatures. The warmer the weather, the slower their brains work.

Cheery Littlebottom   Oh dear.

Shoe   Sir! Look there, sir!

Carrot   Someone's climbing the dunes. Carrying someone.

Vimes   Angua?

Carrot   No sir.

Vimes   Captain. Head straight for the shore there. Men, we're landing. Prepare yourselves to move ashore. We'll be in a foreign land, so take great care.

Lights cross-fade to the submarine.

Nobby   Where are we now, Len?

Leonard of Quirm   On the surface.

Lord Vetinari   We're on *a* surface, gentlemen.

Colon   We're in a cave?

Lord Vetinari   Capital. Well worked out. We're underneath Leshp.

Nobby   It's a lot bigger than a cave. Bigger than a cavern.

Lord Vetinari   At least a couple of miles across. How long will it stay afloat do you think, Leonard?

Leonard of Quirm   Well, the rock has a large proportion of pumice and tufa. Very light. And once floated up, the build up of gas starts to escape very rapidly because of the swell. I don't know. Perhaps a week . . . perhaps another week. And then I think it takes a very long time for a sufficient bubble to build up again.

Nobby What're they saying, Sarge? This island of Leshp *floats*?

Leonard of Quirm A most unusual phenomenon. I'd have thought it was a legend if I hadn't seen it for myself.

Colon Course it's not floating. It's made of rock. Rocks don't float.

Nobby My gran's pumice stone used to float in her bath, Sarge.

Lord Vetinari Fascinating. And did you see the Klatchian fleet on the horizon just before we submerged again? Very well organised. One might almost say . . . *astonishingly* well organised. As they say, 'If you would seek war, prepare for war.'

Leonard of Quirm I believe, my lord, that the saying is, 'If you would seek *peace*, prepare for war.'

Lord Vetinari No. No. Just can't see that one at all. Let us proceed with care. We will go ashore under cover of darkness.

Colon Couldn't we go under cover of *cover*, sir?

Lord Vetinari All those ships will make things much easier. So many different Klatchian races in one place together. We will not stand out so easily.

Colon What about our uniforms? They'd stick out a mile.

Nobby I'm not wandering around in me drawers for no one. Not in a port. Some of them sailors is at sea for a long time.

Colon It's worse than that. Out of uniform, we'd be spies. Oh, well, I don't mind risking it.

Lord Vetinari Well done. Tell me, Sergeant . . . in your long military career, did anyone ever consider promoting you to an officer?

Colon Nossir.

Lord Vetinari I cannot think why.

Blackout.

Scene Two

In the desert.

Vimes *is on stage asleep, tied at the wrists and ankles. It is night. Exterior. A figure in Klatchian robes (***Captain Carrot***) enters, with a dagger, and crosses to him. The figure shakes* **Vimes***.*

Carrot Sir? Sir?

Vimes Wha . . . what? Carrot? Carrot? How did I get here? How did you get here? Why am I tied up?

Carrot Don't you remember, Commander? We were captured. By the D'regs, sir. The second we landed, sir. Despite your warnings to be careful.

Vimes Yes, but why am I tied up when you're wandering around dressed like . . . like El Orange?

Carrot El Orange?

Vimes Yes, yes, you know. He was a Morporkian officer who fought in Klatch years ago on the Klatchians' side. Dressed in their robes and so on. And then he . . . no, hold on, that's not important. *Why* am I tied up?

Carrot They tied us all up at first, sir. I told them to leave you because it was the first chance you'd had for a sleep, sir.

Vimes Oh right. Good thought. But why are we still alive?

Carrot If you're still alive five minutes after meeting D'regs it means they really like you, sir.

He cuts **Vimes***'s bonds.*

Disorganiser   Bingly, Bingly, Beep!

Vimes   Yes?

Disorganiser   Would you like to know about the appointments you missed while you were asleep?

Vimes   No! Captain, why are you wearing a sheet?

Carrot   It's a burnous, sir. Very practical for desert wear. The D'regs gave them to us.

Vimes   Us?

Carrot   The rest of us, sir.

Vimes   Everyone's OK?

Carrot   Oh yes. They only wanted to take us prisoner, sir. One of them did accidentally cut off Constable Shoe's head, sir. But they did help to sew it back on, so that's OK. The D'regs, like all Klatchians, are very hospitable people. They take hospitality very, very, seriously. Ah, sir, this is Jabbar.

Jabbar *enters.*

Jabbar   Offendi.

Carrot   He's their . . . well, he's like an official wise man, sir.

Jabbar   My tent is your tent, offendi.

Vimes   It is?

Jabbar   My wives are your wives.

Vimes (*a little panicky*)   They are? Really?

Jabbar   My food is your food.

He claps his hands. A **Klatchian** *enters carrying a plate of rice and sheep's eyes.* **Jabbar** *takes one.*

The best bit.

Vimes   They look like sheep's eyeballs.

Carrot   Yes sir. But it is unwise to . . .

Vimes You know what? I think this is a little game called 'Let's see what the offendi will swallow.' And I'm not swallowing this, my friend.

Jabbar Then it is true you can see further than most.

Vimes So can this food. My father told me never to eat anything that can wink back.

A pause. Then **Jabbar** *and the* **Klatchian** *laugh.*

Jabbar Well done! Extremely good! First time it not worked in twenty years! Come, we dine on proper rice and lamb.

Vimes We're your prisoners, Jabbar?

Jabbar Honoured guests. My tent is your tent . . .

Vimes But . . . how can I put this? You want us to enjoy your hospitality for some time?

Jabbar We have tradition. A man who is guest in your tent, even if he is your worst enemy, you owe him hospitality for . . . treedace.

Vimes Treedace, eh? Now look, when you captured us we were chasing a man. A Klatchian.

Jabbar I will not speak of this.

The **Klatchian** *exits.* **Jabbar** *moves away from* **Captain Carrot** *and* **Vimes**.

Carrot It's unwise to press them about Ahmed, sir. Look, I had a talk with Jabbar while you were . . . resting. It's a bit political, I'm afraid.

Vimes Hah.

Carrot Prince Cadram is trying to unite the whole of Klatch, you see. But he's been having trouble.

Vimes What kind?

Jabbar Us.

Carrot   None of the tribes like the idea, sir. They've always fought among themselves and now most of them are fighting him. Klatch isn't so much an empire as an argument.

Jabbar   The Prince he say, 'Hey you must be educated. Hey you must pay taxes.' We do not wish to be educated about paying taxes.

Vimes   So you think you're fighting for your freedom?

Carrot   That's a difficult question for a Klatchian, sir. Their word for 'freedom' is the same as their word for 'fighting'.

Vimes   So Prince Cardamom has troubles at home, eh? And does Vetinari know about this?

Carrot   Does a camel shit in the desert, sir?

Jabbar   A man on a horse said we must fight the foreign dogs.

Carrot   That's us, sir.

Jabbar   Because you have stolen an island that is under the sea. What is that to us? We know no harm of you foreign dogs, but the men who oil their beards in Al Khali we do not like. So we send him back.

Vimes   All of him?

Jabbar   We are not barbaric. But we kept the horse.

Vimes   And 71-Hour Ahmed told you to keep us here, didn't he?

Jabbar   No one orders the D'regs! It is our pleasure to keep you here.

Vimes   And when will it be your pleasure to let us go again? When Ahmed tells you?

Jabbar   I will not speak of him. He is devious and cunning and not to be trusted.

Vimes   But he is a D'reg. So are you.

Jabbar   Exactly! We know what we are talking about!
Listen!

Vimes   What?

Jabbar   There is someone out there!

Vimes   Who?

Jabbar (*with a grin*)   We will find out.

Vimes   Why would they attack you now?

Jabbar   Maybe they think we have something that we
want.

Sergeant Detritus *enters.*

Detritus   Sir? What's happening? We could hear some
unexplained movements out there in the desert, Commander.

Vimes   I see the cool desert night air has improved your
intelligence, Sergeant.

Detritus   Immeasurably, Commander.

There is a scream, off. A **Klatchian Captain** *runs on.*

Klatchian Captain   Oh, Jabbar – there is a great dog out
there! I have seen it! It attacks without warning!

Carrot   Angua's out there, sir.

Vimes   But that didn't sound like . . . oh, yes. I see what
you mean.

Carrot   I heard her earlier. She's probably enjoying herself.
She doesn't really get much of a chance to let herself go in
Ankh-Morpork.

Vimes   Er . . . no.

They all peer out into the darkness.

You two getting on all right, are you?

Carrot   Oh, fine, sir. Yes.

Vimes   No . . . problems, then?

Carrot   Oh, not really, sir. She buys her own dog biscuits and she's got her own flap in the door. When it's full moon I don't really get involved.

Corporal Angua *bursts on. She is wearing a loose robe.*

Carrot   Angua!

Angua   There's a couple of hundred soldiers out there! Anyone got any water? And suitable clothes? I got these off . . . well, never mind, but they could've done with a visit to the laundry first.

Jabbar   They will not dare to attack before dawn. At dawn we will attack.

Carrot   Might I suggest an alternative, sir? I have been reading books on tactics, sir. They suggest a good way to deal with overwhelming odds is to turn them into underwhelming odds. Sir.

Vimes   Well?

Carrot   We should attack now.

Jabbar   But it's dark!

Carrot   It's just as dark for the enemy, sir.

Vimes   But it's pitch black! You wouldn't know who the hell you were fighting! Half the time you'd be shooting your own side!

Carrot   *We* wouldn't. Because there's only a few of us, sir. All we need to do is to crawl out there, make a bit of noise and then let them get on with it. All armies are the same size at night, sir.

Angua   There might be something in that. They're crawling around in twos and threes and they're dressed pretty much like . . . (*She indicates* **Jabbar**.)

Carrot   This is Jabbar. He is sort of not their leader.

Angua   Right. I'd like some clean clothes. And a sword, if there's to be fighting.

Carrot   Um, I think the Klatchians have rather specific views about women fighting.

Jabbar   Yes. We expect them to be good at it. We are D'regs. Come on!

Blackout.

Scene Three

A dockside in Klatch.

Night. **Vetinari** *and* **Leonard** *are on stage*

Leonard of Quirm   Smells like home, my lord. But don't trust the water.

Lord Vetinari   I don't trust the water at home, either, Leonard.

Leonard of Quirm   Do you think it was wise, sir?

Lord Vetinari   Mmm?

Leonard of Quirm   Sending Sergeant Colon and Corporal Nobbs off on their own. To recce the area?

Corporal Nobbs *and* **Sergeant Colon** *enter, in long robes and fezzes, carrying a sack.*

Lord Vetinari   Oh, probably not. How did it go, gentlemen?

Colon   Sir? We was robbed, sir.

Lord Vetinari   No! Please, Sergeant, do give us your report.

Colon   Sir. My plan was to get ourselves some Klatchian gear, sir, so's we could merge unnoticed amongst the towelheads, sir. So me and Nob . . . me and Corporal Nobbs lured two blokes into this alley.

Lord Vetinari   And?

Nobby They was thieves, my lord. They beat us up and nicked all our stuff!

Colon Thank you – *Corporal* – I'm giving this report to his lordship. (*He clears his throat.*) We was overwhelmed by overwhelming numbers of villains, sir and they relieved us of our equipment.

Lord Vetinari And then . . . ?

Colon Then we saw some donkeys at the end of the alley, sir. And I instructed Corporal Nobbs to sneak over and whip a couple of sacks of stuff cos, like, they might contain togs, sir . . . or at worst we could've just worn the sacks. But they had good stuff in them, sir.

Lord Vetinari I see. Is that all?

Colon Nossir. We had a near miss with some Klatchian guards, too, sir, what I talked my way out of.

Lord Vetinari Indeed?

Colon Yes, sir. So what are we going to do, sir?

Lord Vetinari We must search out the Klatchian High Command. Thanks to Leonard I have a little . . . package to deliver. I hope it will end the war very quickly.

Now, if there is more suitable clothing in your bag, I will get changed and we can take a look at Al Khali.

He pulls some theatrical props out of the sack, including a sign in Klatchian.

'Gulli, Gulli and Beti – Exotic Tricks and Dances'. Hmm. It would seem that there was a lady among the owners of this sack.

He pulls a sort of harem girl's costume out of the sack.

Nobby What are they?

Lord Vetinari I believe they are called harem pants, Corporal.

Nobby Well, I ain't sure they're going to suit you, my lord.

Lord Vetinari I had not intended that they should suit *me*, Corporal. Please pass me your fez, Corporal Beti.

Blackout.

Scene Four

In the desert.

Vimes *and* **Corporal Angua** *are on stage. Noise of fighting, off.*

Angua It's working, isn't it?

Vimes Yes.

Angua What's he going to do?

Vimes Oh, we'll take their weapons off them and let them go, I expect.

Angua Why do people follow him?

Vimes Well, you're his girlfriend, you ought to know.

Angua That's different. I love him because he's kind without thinking about it. He doesn't watch his own thoughts like other people do. Anyway, I'm a wolf living with people. There's a name for a wolf that lives domestically. If he whistled, I'd come running. It's a bit like you and Lord Vetinari, sir. Sooner or later, we're *all* someone's dog.

Vimes It's like hypnotism. People follow him to see what's going to happen next. It's damned magic.

Angua No. Have you ever watched him? I bet he'd found out everything about Jabbar by the time he'd talked to him for ten minutes. He makes you feel important.

Vimes Politicians do that.

Angua Not the way he does, believe me. Lord Vetinari remembers facts about people, but Carrot takes an *interest*. He takes an interest, so people think they're interesting.

Vimes You're right. He thinks more than I do. Why am I here? Because I'm too stupid to stop and think before I give chase. Even Carrot knew better than to do that. *I'd* have chased after Ahmed's ship without a thought, but *he* knew to report to me first. He did what a responsible officer should do, but me . . . Vetinari's terrier. Chase first, think about it afterwards.

Disorganiser Bingly, Bingly, Beep?

Angua Is that your demon diary?

Vimes Yes, though it seems to be talking about someone else.

Disorganiser Er . . . three p.m., Day Not Filled In. Check Wall Defences.

Vimes See? It thinks I'm still in Ankh-Morpork! It cost Sybil three hundred dollars and it can't even keep track of where I am.

Captain Carrot *rushes on.* **Jabbar** *follows him.*

Carrot I've recruited some of the prisoners into your army, sir.

Vimes We aren't soldiers!

Carrot I thought we were, sir.

Vimes Well yes, we are, in a way. But really we're coppers, like we've always been. We don't kill people unless . . . Hold on, hold on. Jabbar? 'Treedace,' you said. That's *three days!* Seventy-two hours! Seventy-two hours' hospitality — even for your enemy!

Jabbar Yes, offendi?

Vimes So that's why he's called 71-Hour Ahmed.

Jabbar I will not say.

Vimes He told you to keep us here?

Jabbar Yes.

Vimes But not to kill us?

Jabbar Oh, I would not kill my friend Sir Sam Mule.

Vimes Don't give me that rubbish. He wanted time to get somewhere and do something, right?

Jabbar I will not say.

Vimes You don't need to. Because we are *leaving*. And if you kill us – well, 71-Hour Ahmed would not like that, I expect. Carrot!

Carrot Sir?

Vimes We've lost Ahmed. Even Angua can't pick up his trail with the sand blowing all over the place. We're not *needed* here.

Carrot But we *are*, sir. We could help the desert tribes.

Vimes So you want to stay and fight? Against the Klatchians?

Carrot Against the *bad* Klatchians, sir.

Vimes Ah, well, that's the trick, isn't it? Well, you can stay and fight if you like – for the good name of Ankh-Morpork. But I'm off. Okay, Jabbar? You know where he is now, don't you?

Jabbar Yes.

Vimes Tell me.

Jabbar No. I swore to him.

Vimes But D'regs are oath-breakers. Everyone knows that.

Jabbar Oh, oaths, yes. Stupid things. But I gave him my *word*.

Carrot He won't break it, sir.

Jabbar I will not tell you where he is, but I will take you to a place. Where Ahmed can find *you*.

Vimes Very well. But now you may as well tell me. Why 71-Hour Ahmed?

Jabbar He killed a man. In the man's own tent. When he had been his guest for nearly treedace! If he had waited an hour . . .

Vimes Oh, I see. Definitely bad manners. Had the man done anything to deserve it?

Jabbar The man had poisoned a well. Killed an entire village. Even so, to break the tradition of hospitality.

Vimes Yes. I can see that's a terrible thing. Almost . . . impolite.

Jabbar The hour was important. Some things should not be done.

Vimes You're right there, at least. Come on then, Jabbar. Take me to him.

Blackout.

Scene Five

A street in Al Khali.

Crowd. Street scene. **Traders**, *etc.* **Al-Jibla** *moves around the crowd.* **Vetinari** *and* **Sergeant Colon** *enter, wearing the long striped robes and fezzes.* **Corporal Nobbs** *then enters, dressed as a harem girl but still with his huge army boots (pause for laughter).*

Nobby These trousers are bloomin' breezy.

Colon Stop complaining, Nobby. And them boots don't work.

Nobby You kept yours on!

Colon Yeah, but I'm not supposed to be a flower of the desert, am I? A moon of someone else's delight ain't supposed to wear hobnails.

Nobby Hey. I'm not mooning for *anyone's* delight, Sarge.

Lord Vetinari It is vital that we find the whereabouts of the Prince Cadram. Understand?

Al-Jibla (*crossing to them*) Dirty postcards, offendi? Ah, but I see you already have a little treasure of your own.

Nobby Oo're you callin' a treasure?

Colon No thanks, mate, we're . . .

Lord Vetinari . . . strolling entertainers. We were hoping to get an engagement in the Prince's palace . . . perhaps you could help?

Al-Jibla Tall order, offendi. What is it you do?

Lord Vetinari Fire-eating, juggling . . .

Al-Jibla And her?

Lord Vetinari Exotic dancing.

If **Lord Vetinari** *can learn to juggle* **Al-Jibla** *says: 'Jugglers, are you? Well, let's see you juggle, then.'* **Lord Vetinari** *then does so. If* **Lord Vetinari** *can't juggle, then he adds 'magic' to his list and* **Al-Jibla** *says: 'Magic, eh? Show us a trick, then,' and* **Lord Vetinari** *does one or two tricks.*

Lord Vetinari And now, offendi, perhaps my . . . colleagues could invite you for a . . . coffee in yon bar.

Al-Jibla No women in there, entertainer.

Nobby Why not?

Al-Jibla No women asking questions, neither.

Nobby Why not?

Al-Jibla Because it is written, that is why.

Nobby Where'm I supposed to go?

Lord Vetinari Off you go, Beti. And listen for information!

Nobby   I dunno. I only bin a woman for ten minutes and already I hate you male bastards.

He stumps off into the crowds.

Colon   I apologise for Nobby, sir. Don't know what's got into him.

Lord Vetinari   Yes. Well, never mind. Off you go with this man, and learn what you can. (*To* **Colon**.) Our very lives depend upon your appearing to be a stupid fat idiot.

Colon   I ain't very good at acting, sir.

Lord Vetinari   Good. Although an invasion is clearly planned, Prince Cadram will have reserved some forces in case of a land attack. It would be nice to know where they are, because that is where *he* will be.

Sergeant Colon *exits with* **Al-Jibla**. **Vetinari** *exits elsewhere. Crowd movement.*

Lights down, then up again. Another part of the street. **Corporal Nobbs** *re-enters. There is a group of* **Klatchian Women** *to one side of the stage.* **Corporal Nobbs** *stumps on and sits on the ground. One of the women,* **Bana**, *crosses to him . . . er, her . . . er . . .*

Bana   Excuse me, are you the lady who is with the clowns?

Nobby   Er . . . yeah. That's me. Beti.

Bana   My name is Bana. Would you like to come and talk to us? We are trying to comfort Netal. Her betrothed won't marry her tomorrow.

Nobby   The swine!

They cross to the others.

Netal   He wanted to! But he's been taken off to fight in Gebra. All over some island no one's heard of. He said it was his duty.

Nobby   Men!

Mother-in-Law   I expect you'd know a lot about the pleasures of men, then?

Nobby   Who, me? Oh, yeah. Lots.

Bana   You *do?*

Nobby   Why not? Beer's favourite. But you can't beat a good cigar. Long as it's free.

Mother-in-Law   Hah!

Netal   I don't think that is what she meant, Beti.

She whispers in **Corporal Nobbs***'s ear*

Nobby   Oh. That.

Bana   I don't see why men have to go off like this. My betrothed has gone also to Gebra.

Mother-in-Law   I can tell you why. Because it's better than growing watermelons all day. It's better than women.

Netal   Men think war is better than women?

Mother-in-Law   It's always fresh. It's always young. And you can make a good fight last all day.

Bana   But they get killed!

Mother-in-Law   Better to die in battle than in bed, they say.

Sergeant Colon *enters.*

Colon   Nobb . . . erm . . . *Beti*! What are you doing?

Nobby   Nothing, Sar – um, Al.

The girls drift off to join the crowd again as soon as **Sergeant Colon** *enters.*

Nobby   Wait! You don't have to go. (*To* **Colon**.) You know, sometimes I really want to give you a right ding on the head. My first bloody chance for years and you . . .

We hear a donkey braying. The sound comes from the back of the theatre, up high. A crowd has entered and is looking up at a minaret, off.

What's happening?

Klatchian Man Oh no. There's a donkey up the minaret again!

Mother-in-Law It's Valerie!

The crowd groans.

Lord Vetinari Ah, a classic Klatchian problem, Sergeant. Most intriguing.

Colon What's wrong with that? What goes up must come down, eh?

Klatchian Man You don't know? Don't you have minarets in Ur?

Lord Vetinari We have plenty of *donkeys*. (*To* **Colon**.) A narrow, winding staircase and no room to turn around at the top? Oh, any fool can get a donkey *up* a minaret. But have you ever tried to get an animal to go backwards down a narrow spiral staircase in the dark? Can't be done.

Mother-in-Law There's something about a rising staircase. It attracts donkeys. They think there's something at the top.

Klatchian Guard We had to push the last one off the top, right? It splashed.

Mother-in-Law You can't kill Valerie! You'd need at least three men up there and there's no room.

Klatchian Guard Here, I've an idea, offendi. (*To the* **Klatchian Man**.) I can borrow the flying carpet from the palace.

Klatchian Man Is that wise? They were all confiscated because of the war effort.

Klatchian Guard No one will miss it. It's just for a few minutes.

He exits.

Colon What was all that about?

Mother-in-Law   They've gone to get a flying carpet.

Colon   Oh, right. They've got one of them at the University.

Mother-in-Law   You have a University in Ur?

Lord Vetinari   Of course. How do you think Al learned what a donkey looks like?

Laughter.

Perhaps I should *persuade* the donkey to come down?

Klatchian Man   Can't be done, offendi. You can't get past on the stairs, you can't turn it round, and it won't come down backwards.

Lord Vetinari   I shall consider the matter

He exits towards the minaret.

Klatchian Man   This should be good.

Pause.

Needs at least four men. Even then, they'll get kicked black and blue, if they're lucky.

The **Klatchian Guard** *re-enters, carrying a rolled carpet.*

Klatchian Guard   All right, stand clear. Come on, make room.

Mother-in-Law   I can hear hooves.

And so can we, now.

Klatchian Guard   Oh yeah? Like our friend with the fez is getting the donkey down single-handed, right?

Colon   Yes. Sounds like it to me.

Lord Vetinari *re-enters. Either we see just the donkey's head emerge, or a whole donkey if you can run to it.*

Lord Vetinari   There we are. Simple.

Klatchian Man But it can't be done. It's a trick. He had another one in a hidden pocket.

Lord Vetinari (*not in the manner of Tommy Cooper*) Donkey, minaret. Minaret, donkey.

Mother-in-Law Oh thank you, offendi.

She exits to the donkey,

Valerie, Valerie, you silly ass.

Klatchian Guard (*putting down the carpet*) Just like that? It was a trick, yes?

Lord Vetinari Of course it was a trick.

Klatchian Guard Right. So . . . how did you do it?

Lord Vetinari You mean you can't spot it?

Klatchian Man Er . . . you had an inflatable donkey?

Lord Vetinari Can you think of any reason why I would go around with an inflatable donkey? Any reason that you'd care to explain to your dear old white-haired mother?

Klatchian Man Er . . . well, you . . .

The crowd start to exit as they consider the options. **Lord Vetinari** *crosses to the carpet and picks it up.* **Sergeant Colon** *and* **Corporal Nobbs** *watch him.*

Klatchian Guard No, you've got it wrong, it was just the *illusion* of a donkey.

Al-Jibla I think it was a secret compartment in the minaret.

Klatchian Man It was a good illusion, though.

Vetinari *nods to* **Corporal Nobbs** *and* **Sergeant Colon**. *They sneak off.*

Lord Vetinari I think we should go before the guard remembers the carpet. The trouble is, we have transport but we don't know where the army is.

Nobby Gebra, sir. Trust me. It's . . . women's stuff, sir.

Colon Sir, I have to know. How *did* you get that donkey down?

Lord Vetinari Persuasion.

Colon What? Just talking?

Lord Vetinari Yes, Sergeant. Persuasion. And, admittedly, a sharp stick.

Colon Ah . . .

Lord Vetinari The trick of getting donkeys down from minarets, sergeant, is always to find that part of the donkey that seriously *wishes* to get down.

They exit. Just as the lights black out, the **Klatchian Guard** *rushes on again (for his carpet).*

Klatchian Guard Oh no! I am a dead man!

Blackout.

Scene Six

The desert.

Vimes *and* **Jabbar** *are on stage.*

Vimes Right. We're here. What now?

Jabbar Ahmed is watching you.

Vimes I can't see him anywhere.

Jabbar Of course. And I hope we meet again in whatever is your paradise.

He exits.

Vimes Right, er . . .

Disorganiser Bingly, Bingly, Beep!

Vimes Yes? Appointment with 71-Hour Ahmed?

Disorganiser Er . . . no. Klatchian fleet sighted off Ankh-Morpork.

Vimes Is something wrong with you? You're giving me someone else's appointments, you idiot box.

Disorganiser The appointments are correct for Commander Sir Samuel Vimes.

Vimes That's *me*!

Disorganiser But which one of you? Beep.

Vimes *goes to throw it away.* **Ahmed** *has appeared on stage, carrying his sword. He removes his Arab robes to reveal a dinner suit with cream DJ.* **Ahmed** *is now no longer the gravel-voiced grubby D'reg, but speaks like Noël Coward playing James Bond.*

71-Hour Ahmed Sir Samuel. Don't destroy it. It was, after all, a gift of love. Leave your sword, Commander.

Vimes You going to kill me, too? Or is there honour among policemen?

71-Hour Ahmed You do understand. I'm genuinely impressed, Sir Samuel.

Vimes You really fooled me. I really thought you were just . . .

71-Hour Ahmed Just another camel-driver with a towel on his head? Oh dear. And you'd been doing so well up until then. The Prince was most impressed. I consider it a compliment. But don't worry, I wouldn't dream of harming you. Unless you do something . . . foolish.

Vimes You murdered Snowy Slopes, didn't you?

71-Hour Ahmed The term is executed. I can show you the confession that he signed beforehand.

Vimes Of his own free will?

71-Hour Ahmed More or less. I pointed out to him the consequences of not signing the confession. The Assassins'

Guild had a contract on him, anyway. And by a happy chance I *am* a Guild member.

Vimes   You?

71-Hour Ahmed   Oh yes. The best years of my life, they tell me. Up School, up School, right up School! I was in Viper House. I can still recall the taste of that peculiar custard we used to get on Mondays. Dear me, how it all comes back.

Vimes   Why did you drag me here?

71-Hour Ahmed   Drag you? I had to sabotage my own ship so you wouldn't lose me!

Vimes   Yes. But . . . you knew how I'd react. *Everyone* knew how Sam Vimes would react.

71-Hour Ahmed   Cigarette, Commander?

Vimes   I thought you chewed those damned cloves?

71-Hour Ahmed   In Ankh-Morpork, yes. Always be a little bit foreign wherever you are, because everyone knows foreigners are a bit stupid. (*He lights a cigarette in an elegant holder.*) Shall I tell you how I knew that you were a good man, Sir Samuel?

Vimes   Do tell.

71-Hour Ahmed   After the Prince's life I suspected everyone. But you only suspected your own people. You couldn't bring yourself to think Klatchians might have done it. Because that would line you up with Sergeant Colon and all the rest of the 'Klatchian-fags-are-made-of-camel-dung' brigade.

Vimes   Whose policeman are you?

71-Hour Ahmed   Let us say that I draw pay from the Prince Cadram. We thought the same way, Sir Samuel. You thought it was your people, I thought it was mine. The difference is, I was right. Khufurah's death was plotted in Klatch.

Vimes Oh really? That's what they wanted the Watch to think . . .

71-Hour Ahmed *No*, Sir Samuel. The important thing is what someone wanted *you* to think.

Vimes Well, you're wrong there. All the stuff with the broken glass and the sand on the floor. I saw . . . through . . . that . . . straight . . . away.

71-Hour Ahmed (*almost sympathetically*) Yes. You did.

Vimes Damn. I was supposed to see through it, wasn't I?

71-Hour Ahmed Yes, but in some ways you were right. And then someone broke in to Ossie's, making sure they dumped *most* of the glass outside. And distributed the sand. I thought the sand was going too far, too. But they wanted to make it look like a bungled effort.

Vimes Who was it?

71-Hour Ahmed Just some thief.

Vimes Who paid him?

71-Hour Ahmed A man he met in a pub. You see, if the redoubtable Commander Vimes – known even in Klatch to be honest if lacking in intelligence – if even he thinks it was done by his own people . . . well, the world is watching. Starting a war over a rock? Well, that sort of thing makes other countries uneasy. They've all got rocks off their coast. But starting a war because some foreign dog had killed a Prince on a mission of peace? That, I think, the world would understand.

Vimes Lacking in intelligence?

71-Hour Ahmed Oh, don't be depressed, Commander. Listen to me! Prince Cadram ordered his brother's death. What better way to demonstrate the perfidy of the sausage-eaters . . . killing a peacemaker?

Vimes His own brother? You expect me to believe that?

71-Hour Ahmed Messages were sent to the embassy. In code.

Vimes The old ambassador? I don't believe *that*!

71-Hour Ahmed No. You really don't, do you? Be generous, Sir Samuel. Allow Klatchians also to be ruthless, scheming bastards, hmm?

Vimes And where are these messages? In a safe in the embassy, I suppose?

71-Hour Ahmed Oh no. I have them. I . . . liberated them during the fire. But . . . I am Prince Cadram's policeman.

Vimes A death warrant against his own brother. You can't argue against that in court.

71-Hour Ahmed What court? The monarch *is* the law. We are not like you. You kill monarchs.

Vimes The word is 'execute'. And we only did it once. And it was a long time ago. But is that what it's all about? Why all this drama? You could have just come to see me in Ankh-Morpork.

71-Hour Ahmed You are a suspicious man, Commander. Would you have believed me? Besides, I had to get the Prince away before he, ahah, died of his wounds.

Vimes Where is he now?

71-Hour Ahmed Safe. Being looked after by an old woman whom I trust.

Vimes Your mother?

71-Hour Ahmed Ye gods, no! My mother is a D'reg! She would be terribly offended if I trusted her.

Pause.

You think I am a barbarian? Look around you, Commander. Your . . . beat is a city you can walk across in half an hour.

Mine is two million square miles of desert and mountain. My companions are a sword and a camel and, frankly, neither are good conversationalists. It is my job to go into the waste places and chase bandits and murderers five hundred miles from anyone who'd be on my side. So I must inspire dread and strike the first blow because I will not have a chance to strike a second one. I survived seven years in an Ankh-Morpork public school patronised by the sons of gentlemen. Compared to that, life among the D'regs holds no terrors, I assure you. And I administer justice swiftly and inexpensively . . .

Vimes   I heard how you'd got your name.

71-Hour Ahmed   The man had poisoned the water. The only well for twenty miles. That killed five men, seven women, thirteen children and thirty-one camels. And some of them were valuable camels, mark you. I had the evidence.

Vimes   Sometimes we have trials.

71-Hour Ahmed   Yes. Your Lord Vetinari decides. Well, five hundred miles from anywhere the law is me. But what can I do? Arrest my Prince? I am his policeman, as you are Vetinari's.

Vimes   No. I'm an officer of the law. But Prince Cadram – he *wants* a war?

71-Hour Ahmed   Oh, certainly. Nothing unites a country like a good war. A common enemy.

Vimes   A *good* war? Right. *You* are coming with *me*. Push has now come to shove.

Blackout.

Scene Seven

Lord Rust's *encampment.*

Lord Rust, **Lieutenant Hornett** *are on stage, looking out at the army. Noises off.*

Rust   Army looks splendid, Hornett.

Hornett   Yes, sir. If a little less impressive, perhaps, than the army of Klatch.

Rust   Nonsense. General Tacticus was outnumbered ten to one when he took the Pass of Al-Ybi.

Hornett   Yes, sir. Although his army was mounted on elephants, sir. And they had been well provisioned.

Rust   Possibly, possibly. But what about the mere one hundred Ephebians who defeated the entire Tsortean army, eh?

Hornett   Some commentators believe the earthquake helped.

Rust   You will, at least, admit that the Seven Heroes of Hergen beat the Big-Footed People although outnumbered by a hundred to one?

Hornett   Yes, sir. That was a nursery story, sir. It never really happened.

Rust   Are you calling my nanny a liar, boy?

Hornett   No, sir.

Rust   Then you'll concede that Baron Mimbledrone *single-handedly* beat the armies of the Plum Pudding Country and ate their Sultana?

Hornett   I envy him, sir. Sir, Prince Cadram is approaching.

Rust   Excellent. Let us withdraw into my tent so that we can make a better entrance, eh?

Hornett   Yes, sir.

They exit as **Prince Cadram** *and* **General Ashal** *enter.*

Prince Cadram   Is that their entire army?

General Ashal   It would appear so, majesty. But you see, they believe that fortune favours the brave.

Prince Cadram   That is a reason to field such a contemptible little army? And why are we meeting him before the battle?

General Ashal   It's a goodwill gesture, majesty. Warriors honouring one another.

Prince Cadram   But the man's a complete incompetent.

General Ashal   Indeed.

Prince Cadram   So what does he want? For me to say there're no hard feelings?

General Ashal   Basically, yes, majesty. I understand the motto of his old school was: 'It matters not that you won or lost, but that you took part.'

Prince Cadram   And, knowing this, people still take orders from him?

Rust and **Lieutenant Hornett** *enter.*

Rust   Ah, Prince Cadram. Welcome to my camp.

(*We had our* **Cadram** *speak the underlined words in the following speeches in mock-Arabic, with* **Ashal** *producing 'subtitles' with his words in English.*)

Prince Cadram   Tell me, do either of you gentlemen speak Klatchian?

Rust   Er . . . Hornett?

Hornett   I'm not too certain what he said, sir. I can *read* Klatchian, sir, but not . . .

Prince Cadram   Oh, don't worry. As we say in Klatch This clown's in charge of an army?

Rust   Hornett?

Hornett   Er . . . something about . . . to own, to control . . . er . . .

Prince Cadram   I am not familiar with your customs. You often meet your enemies before battle?

Rust   It is considered honourable. On the night before the Battle of Pseudopolis officers from both sides attended a ball at Lady Selachii's, for example.

Prince Cadram   We obviously have much to learn. <u>As the poet Mosheda said, I can't believe this man</u>.

Rust   Ah yes, Klatchian is a very poetic language.

Hornett   Sir, there's something going on. Look, sir – approaching dust.

General Ashal   One moment. (*He pulls out a telescope and looks toward the dust cloud.*) A small army approaches.

Rust   That's a Make-Things-Bigger device, isn't it? My word, you *are* up-to-date. They were only invented last year.

General Ashal   I didn't buy this, Lord Rust. I inherited it from my grandfather. The lead soldiers – they are your Commander Vimes and Captain Carrot!

Rust   What?

Noise of horses approaching. and stopping. **Vimes, Captain Carrot, 71-Hour Ahmed, Corporal Angua, Sergeant Detritus** *and company enter.*

Vimes   Are you Prince Cadram?

Prince Cadram   You too, Ahmed?

71-Hour Ahmed   You're under arrest.

Prince Cadram   I'm what?

71-Hour Ahmed   I am arresting you for conspiracy to murder your brother. There may be other charges.

Prince Cadram   Mr . . . ?

Vimes (*producing his badge*)   Sir Samuel Vimes. Ankh-Morpork City Watch.

Prince Cadram   Well, Sir Samuel, I have only to lift my hand and my bodyguards will cut you down.

71-Hour Ahmed I will kill the first man that moves.

Carrot And I'll kill the second.

Vimes Any volunteers to be the third man?

General Ashal What was that . . . *lie* you uttered about a murder?

Prince Cadram Have you gone mad, Ashal?

General Ashal Oh, I can disbelieve these lies, majesty, but I must know what they are.

Rust Vimes, have you gone mad? You can't arrest the commander of an army!

Carrot Actually, I rather think we can. And the army, too. We could charge them with behaviour likely to cause a breach of the peace, sir. That's what warfare is.

Vimes I *like* it!

Prince Cadram You seriously think you can arrest an entire army? Perhaps you think you have a bigger army?

Vimes Don't need one. Power at a point. And the point is on the tip of Ahmed's crossbow. That wouldn't frighten a D'reg, but you . . . I don't reckon you think like them. Tell your men to stand down.

Prince Cadram Even Ahmed wouldn't shoot his Prince in cold blood.

Vimes (*taking the crossbow*) I wouldn't ask him to. Give that order!

Pause.

Count of three!

General Ashal (*aside, to* **Cadram**) Highness, his ancestor killed the last King of Ankh-Morpork.

Vimes That's right. It runs in the family!

Prince Cadram It would be murder!

Vimes   In wartime? I'm from Ankh-Morpork. We're at war. Can't murder if there's a war on.

One.

General Ashal *whispers to* **Cadram**.

Two.

General Ashal   Theprincewishesmetosay . . .

Vimes   OK, OK, slow down.

General Ashal   Send out the order! Let the messengers leave at once!

Carrot   I'll go and read them their rights, sir.

He exits, with the **Watch**.

Vimes   And the Ankh-Morpork army can stand down as well.

Rust   But Vimes, you're on *our* side . . .

Vimes   Bloody hell, I'm going to shoot *someone* today, Rust, and it could well be you!

Rust   All right. We are 'disarmed'. What now?

Prince Cadram   What now?

Vimes   I'm taking you back to Ankh-Morpork . . .

Rust   You are making a mockery of the whole business, Vimes!

Vimes   So long as I'm doing something right, then.

71-Hour Ahmed   Then you can answer for your crime here, majesty.

Prince Cadram   In what court?

71-Hour Ahmed (*aside, to* **Vimes**)   What was your plan from here on?

Vimes (*aside to* **Ahmed**)   I never thought we'd get this far. (*To* **Cadram**.) We've got proof.

Prince Cadram Really? Fascinating. And to whom will you show this proof, Commander?

Disorganiser Bingly, Bingly, Beep.

Vimes What!?

Disorganiser Seven a.m. Organise defenders at the River Gate. Seven Twenty-Five . . . Hand-to-hand fighting in Peach Pie Street . . . Things to Do Today . . . Build Barricades . . .

71-Hour Ahmed What's that thing talking about?

Vimes It's what would have happened if I hadn't come to Klatch . . . different leg of the trousers of time. You see, if I *hadn't* followed you, then Rust wouldn't have followed *me*. Then Cadram would have invaded Ankh-Morpork and . . .

Prince Cadram Come on, Commander. Do *something*.

Disorganiser Eight-oh-two a.m. . . . Death of Corporal Littlebottom . . . Eight-oh-three a.m. . . . death of Sergeant Detritus . . . Eight-oh-four a.m. . . . Death of Captain Carrot . . .

Prince Cadram They say that in Ankh-Morpork one of your ancestors killed a king. And he also came to no good end.

Vimes I nearly didn't come. I nearly stayed in Ankh-Morpork.

Disorganiser Bingly, Bingly, Beep. Things to Do Today. Die.

Vimes We're in Klatch. I'm a policeman, Prince Cadram. I should follow Klatchian law . . .

He raises the crossbow and points it at **Prince Cadram**. *As he is on the point of firing,* **Lord Vetinari** *enters, carrying a metal tube. He takes the bolt from the bow.*

Lord Vetinari Ah, Vimes. Well done. I see you've got the donkey *up* the minaret. Good morning, gentlemen. I see I am not too late.

Rust   Vetinari? What are you doing here? This is a battlefield.

Lord Vetinari   I wonder. There seem to be a lot of men just sitting around. Many of them are having what I believe soldiers call a brew-up. And Captain Carrot is organising a football match. Besides, I believe that, technically, quite a large number of people are under arrest. So a state of war is not, in fact, in being. It is merely a state of football. Therefore, I believe I am, shall we say . . . back. Excuse me, I won't be a moment.

He starts to open the metal tube. One or two people step back slightly.

Vimes   What's that?

Lord Vetinari   I thought this might become necessary. It took some preparation, but I am certain it will work. We did try to keep the damp off them.

Rolls of paper fall out of the tube. **Vimes** *picks them up.*

Vimes   'Whereas . . . heretofore . . . etc, etc . . . City of Ankh-Morpork . . . *surrender?*'

Rust *and* **Prince Cadram**   WHAT??

Lord Vetinari   Yes, surrender. A little piece of paper and it's all over. I think you'll find it's all in order.

Rust   You can't . . .

Prince Cadram   You can't . . .

General Ashal   Unconditionally?

Lord Vetinari   Yes, I think so. We give up all claim to Leshp in favour of Klatch. We will withdraw our troops from Klatch and our citizens from Leshp. And, say, half a million dollars in reparation? We should sign the document on neutral territory, though. Not Ankh-Morpork, of course . . .

General Ashal   What about Leshp?

Lord Vetinari   Oh yes. I would never have thought of that.

Prince Cadram   But that is *ours*!

General Ashal   *Will* be, majesty. Once the document has been signed.

Prince Cadram   Half a million is not enough.

Lord Vetinari   We can discuss it.

Rust   You will answer for this in Ankh-Morpork, Vetinari!

Lord Vetinari   No doubt. Now . . . shall we proceed inside to conclude our discussions?

Vimes   But what about my arrest? I'm not . . .

Lord Vetinari   There are larger issues here.

Vimes   But . . .

Lord Vetinari   Sterling work, nonetheless.

Vimes   There are big crimes and little crimes. Is that it?

Lord Vetinari   Now, alas, it is a time for men of words. Enjoy the sunshine. We shall be returning home shortly. (*To the others.*) Shall we . . . ?

Vetinari, Rust, Lieutenant Hornett, Cadram *and* **General Ashal** *exit. Only* **Vimes** *and* **Ahmed** *remain.*

71-Hour Ahmed   That's your master, is it?

Vimes   No. He's just the man who pays my wages! What'll happen to *you*? *Your* boss isn't going to be too pleased with you.

71-Hour Ahmed   Oh, the desert can swallow me.

Vimes   He'll send people after you.

71-Hour Ahmed   The desert will swallow *them*, too. And now, I think, I shall head that way. There are thieves up in the mountains. There the air is clear. As you know, there is always work for policemen.

Vimes   You thinking of returning to Ankh-Morpork any time?

71-Hour Ahmed   You'd like to see me there, Sir Samuel?

Vimes   It's an open city. Call in at the Watch House when you arrive.

71-Hour Ahmed   Ah, and we can reminisce about old times.

Vimes   No. So you can hand over that sword.

71-Hour Ahmed   I'd take some persuading, Sir Samuel.

Vimes   Oh, I only think I'd ask once.

Ahmed *laughs. They shake hands and walk off in opposite directions as the lights black out.*

Scene Eight

The Rats' Chamber, Ankh-Morpork.

Onstage are various dignitaries, including **Lord Rust**. *Also on are* **Captain Carrot**, **Corporal Angua**, **Sergeant Colon**, **Corporal**s **Nobbs** *and* **Littlebottom**, *and* **Sergeant Detritus**. **Vetinari** *enters, in manacles, accompanied by* **Vimes**.

Lord Vetinari   I'm sure I should be wearing more chains.

Vimes   Are you sure you're taking this seriously, sir?

Lord Vetinari   Oh yes. (*To the assembled throng.*) Can we make this quick? It's going to be a busy day.

Rust   This is not a formal trial, Vetinari. It is an arraignment so that the charges may be known. Slant will read the charges . . .

Lord Vetinari   Shall we get on with it?

Slant   Lord Vetinari, in a nutshell, you are charged with treason. You surrendered most ignobly . . .

Lord Vetinari   But I did not.

Slant   . . . and quite illegally waived all rights to our sovereignty of the country known as Leshp . . .

Lord Vetinari But there is no such place.

Rust Are you quite sane, sir? We were there.

Lord Vetinari The surrender terms were to be ratified on the island of Leshp. But there is no such place.

Rust We passed it on the way back here, man!

Lord Vetinari Have you checked recently? Sergeant?

Angua It's true. At his Lordship's suggestion, I went there yesterday with Captain Jenkins. There was nothing but some floating debris. The island appears to have sunk again.

Rust Did you know about this?

Lord Vetinari How could I possibly know? All I know, Lord Rust, is that Prince Cadram has, at a politically dangerous time for him, given up a huge military advantage in exchange for an island which seems to have sunk under the sea. The Klatchians are a proud people. I wonder what they will think?

Rust You knew! You knew all the time!

Vimes Is Lord Vetinari charged with anything?

Slant Not . . . as . . . such.

Vimes *removes the manacles.*

Lord Vetinari Splendid. And now, ladies and gentlemen, do not let me detain you any further. I have a city to run.

The dignitaries and the **Watch** *file out.* **Vetinari**, **Vimes** *and* **Captain Carrot** *remain.*

Lord Vetinari Now. First, I have drafted a proclamation for the town criers. The news is good.

Carrot The war is officially over, is it, my lord?

Lord Vetinari The war, Captain, never happened. It was a . . . misunderstanding.

Vimes A misunderstanding? People got killed! What about the Prince?

Lord Vetinari   Oh, I am sure we can do business with him, Vimes.

Vimes   I don't think so!

Lord Vetinari   Prince Khufurah? I thought you liked him, Vimes.

Vimes   What? What happened to the other one?

Lord Vetinari   He appears to have left for a long visit to the country. At some speed. He seems to have upset people.

Lady Ramkin *enters.*

Lord Vetinari   Lady Sybil? How nice to see you.

Vimes   Sybil?

Lady Ramkin   Hello, Sam.

Lord Vetinari   I am particularly glad that Lady Sybil is here to hear this. I am persuaded to change the title of your office.

Vimes   Yes?

Lord Vetinari   'Commander' is rather a mouthful. So I have been reminded that a word that originally meant 'commander' was 'dux'.

Vimes   Dux Vimes? *Duke?* Oh no. No way.

Lord Vetinari   There are associated matters.

Vimes   I won't have this, my lord!

Lord Vetinari   Perhaps you should hear them.

Vimes   No! You've done this to me before! We've got the Watch set up, we've almost got the numbers, the dartboard we've got is nearly new. You can't bribe me into accepting this time! There is *nothing* we want!

Lord Vetinari   Stoneface Vimes was a much-maligned man, I've always thought.

Vimes   I'm not accepting . . . what?

Carrot I've always thought so too, my lord. He acted in the best interests of the city when he beheaded the last king.

Lord Vetinari The thought occurs to me that this might be the time for . . . reconsideration of certain ancient assumptions.

Vimes You're offering to rewrite history?

Lord Vetinari Oh, my dear Vimes, history changes all the time. It is constantly being re-examined and re-evaluated, otherwise how would we keep historians occupied? The Chairman of the Guild of Historians is in full agreement with me, I know, that the pivotal role of your ancestor in the city's history is ripe for . . . analysis.

Vimes Discussed it with him, have you?

Lord Vetinari Not yet. And, of course, other details would have to be taken care of.

Vimes Such as?

Lord Vetinari The Vimes coat of arms would be resurrected, of course. I know Lady Sybil was very upset when she found you weren't entitled to one.

Lady Ramkin That's true, Sam. You'll be entitled to a coronet, too.

Lord Vetinari Which you can wear on formal occasions, such as, for example, the unveiling of a statue which has so far disgraced the city by its absence.

Vimes Old Stoneface again? A statue to Old Stoneface?

Lord Vetinari Well done. Not of you, obviously. Putting up a statue to someone who tried to *stop* a war is not very, um, statuesque. Of course, if you had butchered five hundred of your own men out of arrogant carelessness, we'd be melting the bronze already. No, I was thinking of the first Vimes who tried to make a future and merely made history. I thought perhaps somewhere in Peach Pie Street . . .

Vimes Top of Broad Way. Right in front of the palace.

Lord Vetinari   Agreed. I shall enjoy looking at it.

Vimes   All right, then. But I thought only a king could make someone a duke . . . (*He looks from* **Vetinari** *to* **Captain Carrot**.)

Lord Vetinari   I'm sure, if ever there is a king in Ankh-Morpork again, he will choose to ratify my decision. And if there never is, well then there are no practical problems.

Vimes   I'm bought and sold, aren't I? Bought and sold.

Lord Vetinari   Not at all.

Vimes   Yes I am. We all are. Even Rust. And all those poor buggers who went off to get slaughtered. We're not part of the big picture, right? We're just bought and sold.

Lord Vetinari (*irritated and about as angry as he would let himself get*)   Really? Men marched away, Vimes. But men marched *back*. How glorious would have been the battles they never had to fight? And you say bought and sold? All right. But not, I think, *needlessly spent.*

He smiles, briefly.

Veni, Vidi . . . Vetinari.

Blackout.

Other Discworld novels adapted by Stephen Briggs
and available from Methuen

TERRY PRATCHETT

GOING POSTAL

Adapted for the stage by Stephen Briggs

TERRY PRATCHETT

Adapted for the stage by Stephen Briggs

NIGHT WATCH

TERRY
PRATCHETT
Adapted for the stage by Stephen Briggs
MONSTROUS
REGIMENT

TERRY PRATCHETT

Adapted for the stage by
Stephen Briggs

THE FIFTH ELEPHANT